contents

How to use this book	3
5-digit numbers	4–8
Adding 4-digit numbers	9–11
Add and subtract 2- and 3-digit numbers	12–15
Mental subtraction of 3- and 4-digit numbers	16–18
Mental word problems	19–21
Two decimal places	22–26
Mental multiplication strategies	27–29
12- and 24-hour clock	30–32
Length and perimeter	33–37
Subtracting 3-digit numbers	38–42
Subtracting 3- and 4-digit numbers by counting up	43–44
Finding change by counting up	45–46
Multiples and factors	47–49
Comparing fractions and finding equivalents	50–54
Multiplying 3- and 4-digit numbers by 1-digit numbers	55–59
Dividing 3-digit numbers by 1-digit numbers	60–63
Measuring angles	64–68
Circles	69–72

Rounding 5-digit numbers	**73–74**
Rounding and ordering decimals	**75–78**
Comparing fractions and decimals	**79–81**
Addition and subtraction: mental strategies and written methods	**82–86**
Multiplication and division: mental strategies and written methods	**87–90**
Identifying operations	**91–92**
Practising calculations	**93**
Number puzzles	**94–95**

Key

Number and Place value

Addition and Subtraction

Multiplication and Division

Shape, Data and Measure

Fractions and Decimals

Mixed Operations

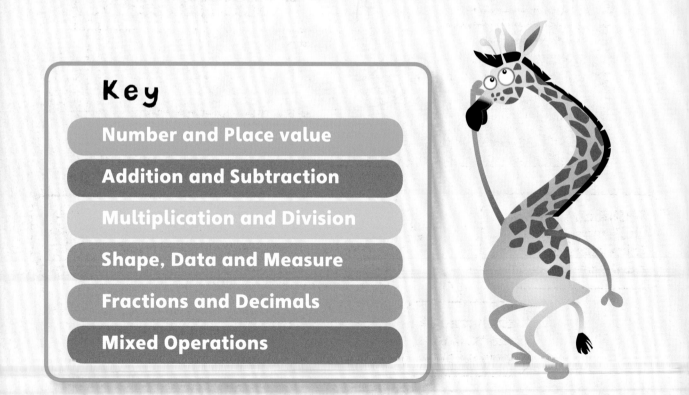

How to use this book

The first page of each section will have a title telling you what the next few pages are about.

Some pages will show you an example or model.

Your teacher may tell you to GRAB something that might help you answer the questions.

Read the instructions carefully before each set of questions.

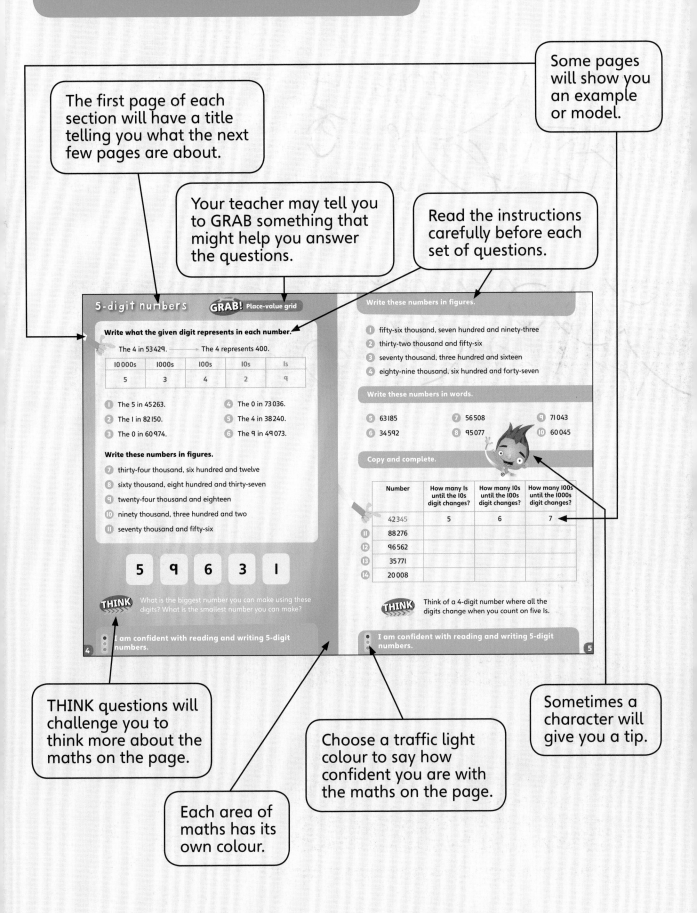

THINK questions will challenge you to think more about the maths on the page.

Sometimes a character will give you a tip.

Choose a traffic light colour to say how confident you are with the maths on the page.

Each area of maths has its own colour.

5-digit numbers

 GRAB! Place-value grid

Write what the given digit represents in each number.

The 4 in 53 429. ⟶ The 4 represents 400.

10 000s	1000s	100s	10s	Is
5	3	4	2	9

1. The 5 in 45 263.
2. The I in 82 150.
3. The 0 in 60 974.

4. The 0 in 73 036.
5. The 4 in 38 240.
6. The 9 in 49 073.

Write these numbers in figures.

7. thirty-four thousand, six hundred and twelve
8. sixty thousand, eight hundred and thirty-seven
9. twenty-four thousand and eighteen
10. ninety thousand, three hundred and two
11. seventy thousand and fifty-six

5	9	6	3	I

 **THINK** What is the biggest number you can make using these digits? What is the smallest number you can make?

⬤ **I am confident with reading and writing 5-digit**
◯ **numbers.**
◯

Write these numbers in figures.

1. fifty-six thousand, seven hundred and ninety-three
2. thirty-two thousand and fifty-six
3. seventy thousand, three hundred and sixteen
4. eighty-nine thousand, six hundred and forty-seven

Write these numbers in words.

5. 63 185
6. 34 592
7. 56 508
8. 95 077
9. 71 043
10. 60 045

Copy and complete.

	Number	How many Is until the 10s digit changes?	How many 10s until the 100s digit changes?	How many 100s until the 1000s digit changes?
	42 345	5	6	7
11	88 276			
12	96 562			
13	35 771			
14	20 008			

THINK   Think of a 4-digit number where all the digits change when you count on five Is.

● I am confident with reading and writing 5-digit
○ numbers.
○

1 50 000 + 2000 + 100 + 40 + 9 = ☐

2 60 000 + 7000 + 300 + 30 + 4 = ☐

3 80 000 + ☐ + 70 + 2 = 85 072

4 3982 – ☐ = 3082

5 90 000 + 700 + 50 + 1 = ☐

6 80 + 2 + 5000 + 20 000 + 100 = ☐

7 42 345 – 300 = ☐

8 700 + 40 + 90 000 + 9 = ☐

9 36 213 – ☐ = 30 213

10 24 575 – ☐ = 24 075

8000   500

30 000   1

20

Write answers for each pair.

11 3450 + 200 = ☐

3450 – 200 = ☐

12 23 932 + 30 = ☐

23 932 – 30 = ☐

13 46 932 + 2001 = ☐

46 932 – 2001 = ☐

14 60 503 + 402 = ☐

60 503 – 402 = ☐

I am confident with place value in 5-digit numbers.

6

Write the missing number for each addition and subtraction.

1 23 216 + 2100 = ☐

2 53 482 – 280 = ☐

3 45 834 + 3004 = ☐

4 23 346 + ☐ = 29 347

5 53 671 – 3500 = ☐

6 92 078 + ☐ = 93 088

7 44 277 + 4020 = ☐

8 67 807 + ☐ = 67 909

9 83 162 – 10 060 = ☐

10 56 778 – ☐ = 46 779

11 21 897 – ☐ = 20 807

12 84 713 + ☐ = 84 784

13 92 275 – ☐ = 82 175

14 66 256 + 2110 = ☐

15 35 504 + ☐ = 36 644

16 53 022 + 724 = ☐

17 45 427 – ☐ = 40 117

18 32 208 + 11 101 = ☐

19 57 642 + ☐ = 59 752

20 5213 + 20 103 = ☐

 **THINK** A number plus 11 001 has the answer 47 829.
What is the same number minus 11 001?

● I am confident with solving place-value additions
○ and subtractions for 5-digit numbers.

7

Write > or < between each pair of numbers.

1. 4785   5865
2. 3672   7631
3. 7835   8201
4. 8114   4799
5. 4285   4386

6. 5249   5832
7. 1536   1387
8. 9089   9102
9. 3113   3047
10. 7354   7381

Write > or < between each pair of 5-digit numbers.

11. 47 384   32 562
12. 58 588   84 294
13. 62 789   65 893
14. 76 113   73 285
15. 81 539   87 444
16. 35 675   36 042
17. 75 943   75 246
18. 58 742   58 698

 Write three numbers that lie between 49 243 and 49 803.

I am confident with comparing 5-digit numbers.

Adding 4-digit numbers

$$\begin{array}{r} 4382 \\ + 591 \\ \hline \end{array}$$

Estimate... 5000

$$\begin{array}{r} 4382 \\ + 591 \\ 1 \\ \hline 4973 \end{array}$$

Use the method above to find the totals. Estimate first.

1
$$\begin{array}{r} 4728 \\ + 158 \\ \hline \end{array}$$

2
$$\begin{array}{r} 5836 \\ + 523 \\ \hline \end{array}$$

3
$$\begin{array}{r} 9469 \\ + 121 \\ \hline \end{array}$$

4
$$\begin{array}{r} 7667 \\ + 514 \\ \hline \end{array}$$

5
$$\begin{array}{r} 4728 \\ + 5258 \\ \hline \end{array}$$

6
$$\begin{array}{r} 3622 \\ + 3658 \\ \hline \end{array}$$

7
$$\begin{array}{r} 4045 \\ + 6158 \\ \hline \end{array}$$

8
$$\begin{array}{r} 6307 \\ + 5756 \\ \hline \end{array}$$

9
$$\begin{array}{r} 4543 \\ + 7258 \\ \hline \end{array}$$

10
$$\begin{array}{r} 9753 \\ + 2689 \\ \hline \end{array}$$

○
○ **I am confident with adding 4-digit numbers using**
○ **the column method.**

Look at the additions below.

1 Which of these do you think will give the largest answer?

2 Which will give the smallest answer?

3 Which will give the answer closest to 10 000?

Find the totals, estimating first.

4
```
   3864
 + 4058
 _____
```

3864 to the nearest thousand is 4000.

4000 + 4000 = 8000

5
```
   6846
 + 4822
 _____
```

6
```
   7488
 + 4174
 _____
```

7
```
   8961
 + 8054
 _____
```

8
```
   6668
 + 5158
 _____
```

9
```
   5722
 + 7638
 _____
```

10
```
   7045
 + 6358
 _____
```

11
```
   1369
 + 5756
 _____
```

12
```
   1426
 + 8658
 _____
```

13
```
   3755
 + 2689
 _____
```

THINK Work out the missing digits:

```
     2 5 7 6
 + [ ][ ][ ][ ]
 _____
     6 3 1 7
```

I am confident with adding 4-digit numbers using the column method.

Some animals entered a contest. Add the votes to find out their scores.

1 Skateboarding cat

```
   3564
   3252
+  4053
-------
```

2 Whispering horse

```
   2745
   5352
+  4353
-------
```

3 Ice-skating mouse

```
   3816
   1846
+  4750
-------
```

4 Talking dog

Hi!

```
   4722
   1846
+  6631
-------
```

5 Skipping frog

```
   1647
   3846
+  3738
-------
```

6 Dancing mole

```
   5868
    986
+  6415
-------
```

7 Jumping cow

```
   4527
   4635
+  4258
-------
```

8 Hang-gliding hamster

```
   2738
   8452
+  2364
-------
```

9 Swimming bird

```
   8352
    635
+  1258
-------
```

10 Which animal won the contest?

 **THINK** How many votes did the skateboarding cat and the talking dog get altogether?

I am confident with adding 4-digit numbers using the column method.

Add and subtract 2- and 3-digit numbers

1 37 + 59 = ☐

2 28 + 57 = ☐

3 94 − 68 = ☐

4 44 + 89 = ☐

5 57 + 63 = ☐

6 68 + 72 = ☐

7 77 − 36 = ☐

8 163 − 58 = ☐

9 267 + 31 = ☐

10 472 − 39 = ☐

11 57 + 259 = ☐

12 836 − 63 = ☐

13 75 + 754 = ☐

14 848 − 62 = ☐

15 381 + 79 = ☐

16 837 − 59 = ☐

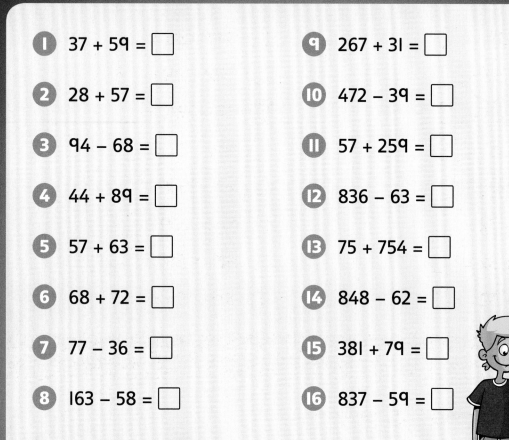

Solve these problems.

17 James is 93 cm tall. James is 58 cm shorter than his brother. How tall is his brother?

18 A coat was reduced in a sale by £37. If it cost £81 before the sale, what was its sale price?

19 Amira has a bowl of cream. She puts 325 ml of it in a cake. Then she gives the 78 ml left in the bowl to her cat. How much cream did Mel have to start with?

20 The summit of a mountain is 853 m above sea level. Clive is 88 m beneath the summit. How many metres above sea level is Clive?

○ **I am confident with addition and subtraction of**
○
○ **2- and 3-digit numbers.**

Complete these additions and subtractions.

1. 77 + 59 = ☐
2. 94 – 67 = ☐
3. 62 – 28 = ☐
4. 86 + 79 = ☐
5. 87 – 63 = ☐
6. 168 – 72 = ☐
7. 377 + 36 = ☐
8. 123 – 78 = ☐

9. 477 + 36 = ☐
10. 422 – 39 = ☐
11. 57 + 289 = ☐
12. 816 – 67 = ☐
13. 67 + 738 = ☐
14. 848 – 69 = ☐
15. 981 + 59 = ☐
16. 817 – 66 = ☐

Solve these problems.

17. What number is 83 more than 47?

18. Lena is 67 years younger than her grandma. How old would her grandma be when Lena is 28?

19. Hassan does a survey of birds. He sees 117 birds in the morning and 68 in the afternoon. How many more did he see in the morning than in the afternoon?

20. Jo puts 364 g of flour, 48 g of sugar and 75 g of butter into a bowl and mixes it. What is the mass of the mixture?

21. Jake is 26 years younger than his dad. Jake's grandad is 23 years older than Jake's dad. Jake is 9 years old, how old is his grandad?

THINK How many different ways can you write an addition of two 2-digit numbers to get the answer 147? Write at least four.

I am confident with addition and subtraction of 2- and 3-digit numbers.

Use place value to add or subtract.

300 7
60 5000

1 5367 − 307 = ☐

3 3639 − 2200 = ☐

2 4224 + 501 = ☐

4 4357 + 621 = ☐

Count on to complete these additions.

5 835 + 43 = ☐

7 684 + 35 = ☐

6 356 + 37 = ☐

8 556 + 76 = ☐

Use Frog to complete these subtractions.

9 134 − 88 = ☐

11 153 − 78 = ☐

10 143 − 96 = ☐

12 321 − 284 = ☐

Count back to complete these subtractions.

13 174 − 25 = ☐

15 363 − 35 = ☐

14 243 − 28 = ☐

16 573 − 61 = ☐

Partition to add or subtract.

17 47 + 85 = ☐

19 89 − 45 = ☐

18 56 + 67 = ☐

20 79 − 36 = ☐

Use known number facts to add or subtract.

21 175 − 6 = ☐

23 382 − 8 = ☐

22 286 + 8 = ☐

24 435 + 7 = ☐

I am confident with mental addition and subtraction of 2- and 3-digit numbers using different methods.

Choose a good method for completing each addition or subtraction.

1. 4357 + 1202 = ☐
2. 123 – 78 = ☐
3. 382 – 7 = ☐
4. 573 – 61 = ☐
5. 4824 – 504 = ☐
6. 79 – 35 = ☐
7. 356 + 27 = ☐
8. 116 – 88 = ☐
9. 834 – 55 = ☐
10. 72 – 47 = ☐
11. 553 – 38 = ☐
12. 67 + 75 = ☐
13. 784 + 33 = ☐
14. 135 – 91 = ☐
15. 546 + 86 = ☐
16. 321 – 284 = ☐

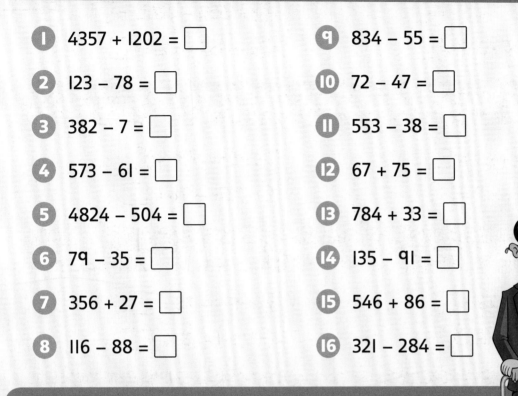

Solve these problems.

17. The tallest man ever to live, Robert Wadlow, was 272 cm tall. Tom is 94 cm shorter than this. How tall is Tom?

18. The Roman Emperor Antonius Pius began his reign in the year 138 AD. After 23 years he died. In what year did he die?

19. Sam had £78 in his money box. He took out £27 and bought a new jumper. He now wants to buy a new phone, which costs £95. How much more money does he now need to save?

20. In 1976 the Olympic Games were held in Canada. In 1924 they were held in France. How many years apart are these two dates?

I am confident with mental addition and subtraction of 2- and 3-digit numbers using appropriate methods.

Mental subtraction of 3- and 4-digit numbers

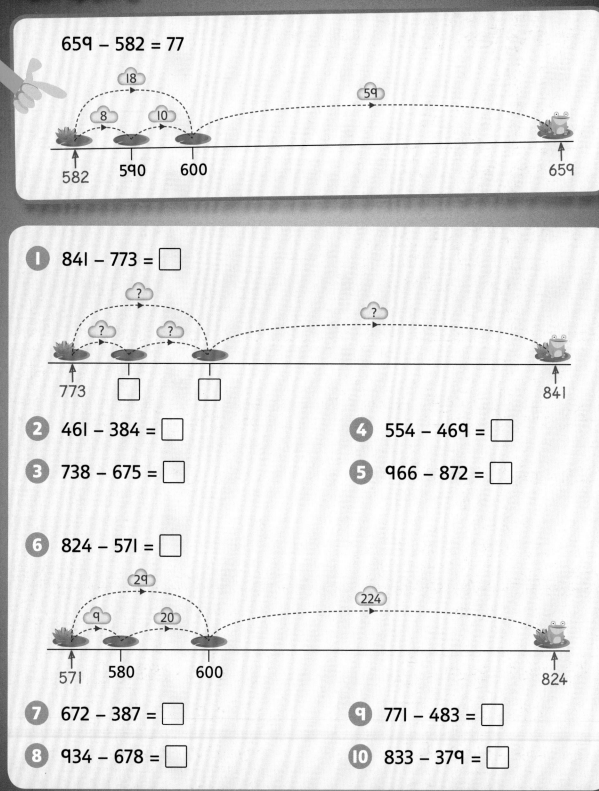

659 – 582 = 77

18
8   10
59
582   590   600   659

1. 841 – 773 = ☐

?
?   ?
?
773   ☐   ☐   841

2. 461 – 384 = ☐

3. 738 – 675 = ☐

4. 554 – 469 = ☐

5. 966 – 872 = ☐

6. 824 – 571 = ☐

29
9   20
224
571   580   600   824

7. 672 – 387 = ☐

8. 934 – 678 = ☐

9. 771 – 483 = ☐

10. 833 – 379 = ☐

○ I am confident with subtraction of 3-digit numbers
using the mental method of counting up.

16

1 729 − 584 = ☐

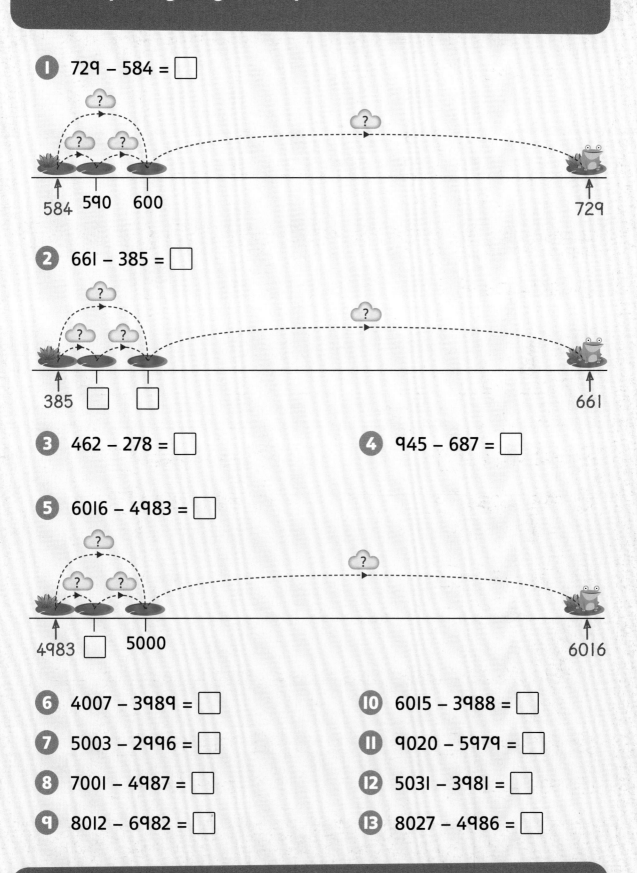

584   590   600   729

2 661 − 385 = ☐

385   ☐   ☐   661

3 462 − 278 = ☐   **4** 945 − 687 = ☐

5 6016 − 4983 = ☐

4983   ☐   5000   6016

6 4007 − 3989 = ☐   **10** 6015 − 3988 = ☐

7 5003 − 2996 = ☐   **11** 9020 − 5979 = ☐

8 7001 − 4987 = ☐   **12** 5031 − 3981 = ☐

9 8012 − 6982 = ☐   **13** 8027 − 4986 = ☐

○ **I am confident with subtraction of 3- and 4-digit**
○ **numbers using the mental method sof counting up.**

1   704
      − 689

2   800
      − 769

3   1001
      − 875

4   2000
      − 967

5   2000
      − 1978

6   5000
      − 3975

7   8002
      − 5889

8   7000
      − 3894

9   9000
      − 6945

10   7002
      − 5964

11   5002
      − 3897

12   8010
      − 3788

13   9013
      − 4867

14   6006
      − 2858

15   9000
      − 5446

THINK   A pair of 4-digit numbers have a difference of 1025. One number is above 7000 and the other is below 6000. Write different possible numbers that the pair could be.

I am confident with subtraction of 3- and 4-digit numbers using the mental method sof counting up.

Mental word problems

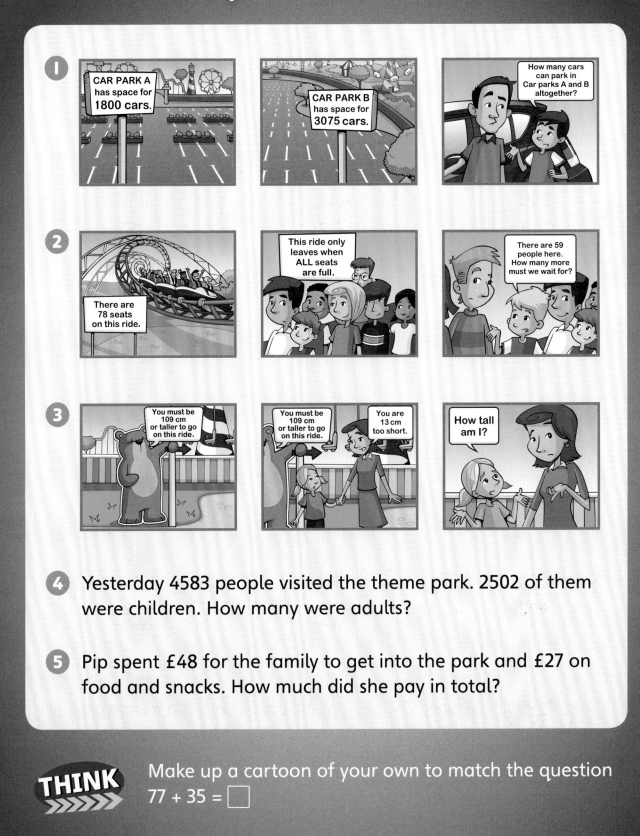

4 Yesterday 4583 people visited the theme park. 2502 of them were children. How many were adults?

5 Pip spent £48 for the family to get into the park and £27 on food and snacks. How much did she pay in total?

THINK Make up a cartoon of your own to match the question
77 + 35 = ☐

○
○ **I am confident with addition and subtraction word**
○ **problems using mental methods.**

19

1. Anton is a scientist. He pours 74 ml of acid into a test tube. How much more does he need to add to make 100 ml?

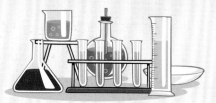

2. In an experiment, Anton must shake a mixture for 25 seconds and then wait for a further 37 seconds. How many seconds will this take altogether?

3. Anton weighs a bowl full of sodium. The scales show 3258 g. If the bowl weighs 1021 g, how much does the sodium weigh?

4. He has two containers. One holds 2000 ml and the other holds 725 ml. How much more does the larger container hold?

5. A saucer held 138 ml of water. After several days of evaporation it held 86 ml. How much water had evaporated?

6. There are 500 scientists who work at a centre. This month, 378 of them got a pay rise. How many did not?

7. Into a bowl weighing 1021 g, Anton puts 203 g of powder and 610 g of salt. He puts the bowl onto the scales. What weight is shown?

8. At the centre there are 500 scientists, 214 support staff, 52 cleaners and 30 canteen workers. How many people work at the centre in total?

I am confident with addition and subtraction word problems using mental methods.

Solve these word problems.

1. Mr Smith and Mr Barr are on a plane. Mr Barr says that he has been on 73 flights in his life. Mr Smith says that it is his 47th flight. How many more flights has Mr Barr been on?

2. A plane is on a 2000 km flight. After I hour it has flown 482 km. How many more kilometres does it have to go?

3. Of the 304 passengers on a plane, 268 are adults and the rest are children. How many are children?

4. On a plane 57 chicken meals and 74 vegetarian meals were served. How many meals were served altogether?

5. A pilot flew 2621 km on Monday and 3053 km on Tuesday. How far did she fly altogether?

6. On a plane there are 154 men, 142 women and 9 children. How many people are on the plane?

7. A plane has 248 seats, of which 67 are empty and 8 are being used by the airline staff. The rest of the seats are taken by passengers. How many passengers are there?

8. There are 1000 passengers at a Greek airport about to fly to London, Manchester or Birmingham. 295 are going to London and 304 are going to Manchester. How many are going to Birmingham?

I am confident with addition and subtraction word problems using mental methods.

GRAB! A place-value grid

Write what the given digit represents in each number.

The 5 in 37·05. The 5 represents five hundredths, or five 0·01s or 0·05.

100s	10s	1s		0·1s	0·01s
	3	7	·	0	5

1 The 2 in 47·21.

2 The 3 in 63·87.

3 The 1 in 79·1.

4 The 6 in 22·36.

5 The 0 in 37·05.

6 The 8 in 383·29.

7 The 6 in 137·61.

8 The 9 in 245·19.

Write a number where:

9 the tenths digit is two more than the tens digit.

10 the hundredths digit is one less than the tenths digit.

11 the tens digit is five more than the hundredths digit.

12 the hundreds digit is double the hundredths digit.

13 the tenths digit is three times the tens digit.

THINK A number less than 50 has a hundredths digit. The tenths digit and the ones digits have a total that is the same as the tens digit. If the number has no zero digits, what could it be? Find four different answers.

I am confident with place value of decimals to two decimal places.

Write the outputs for each input.

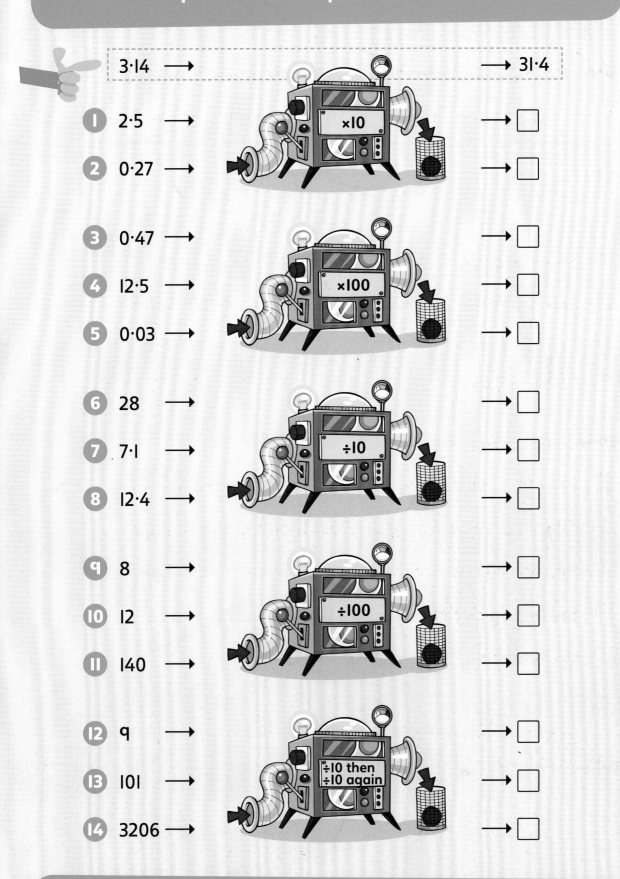

3·14 ⟶ ⟶ 31·4

1 2·5 ⟶ [×10] ⟶ ☐

2 0·27 ⟶ ⟶ ☐

3 0·47 ⟶ ⟶ ☐

4 12·5 ⟶ [×100] ⟶ ☐

5 0·03 ⟶ ⟶ ☐

6 28 ⟶ ⟶ ☐

7 7·1 ⟶ [÷10] ⟶ ☐

8 12·4 ⟶ ⟶ ☐

9 8 ⟶ ⟶ ☐

10 12 ⟶ [÷100] ⟶ ☐

11 140 ⟶ ⟶ ☐

12 9 ⟶ ⟶ ☐

13 101 ⟶ [÷10 then ÷10 again] ⟶ ☐

14 3206 ⟶ ⟶ ☐

I am confident with place-value multiplications and divisions involving decimals.

Write the missing outputs or inputs.

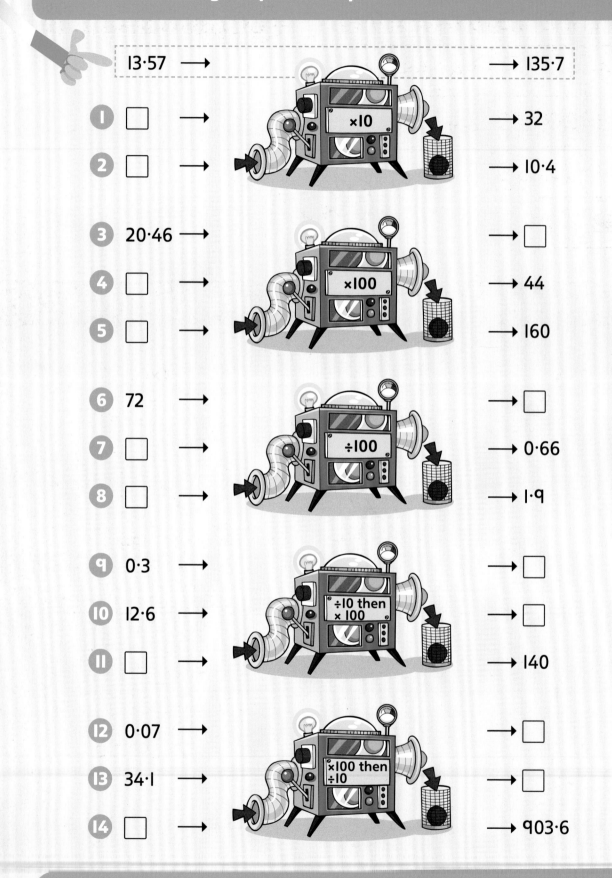

13·57 ⟶ ⟶ 135·7

×10

1 ☐ ⟶ ⟶ 32

2 ☐ ⟶ ⟶ 10·4

3 20·46 ⟶ ⟶ ☐

×100

4 ☐ ⟶ ⟶ 44

5 ☐ ⟶ ⟶ 160

6 72 ⟶ ⟶ ☐

÷100

7 ☐ ⟶ ⟶ 0·66

8 ☐ ⟶ ⟶ 1·9

9 0·3 ⟶ ⟶ ☐

÷10 then × 100

10 12·6 ⟶ ⟶ ☐

11 ☐ ⟶ ⟶ 140

12 0·07 ⟶ ⟶ ☐

×100 then ÷10

13 34·1 ⟶ ⟶ ☐

14 ☐ ⟶ ⟶ 903·6

● I am confident with place-value multiplications
○ and divisions involving decimals.
○

0.1	0.2	0.3	0.4	0.5	0.6
1.1	1.2	1.3	1.4	1.5	
2.1	2.2	2.3	2.4		
3.1	3.2	3.3			
4.1	4.2				

3.4

4.3 | 4.4

Copy and complete on squared paper.

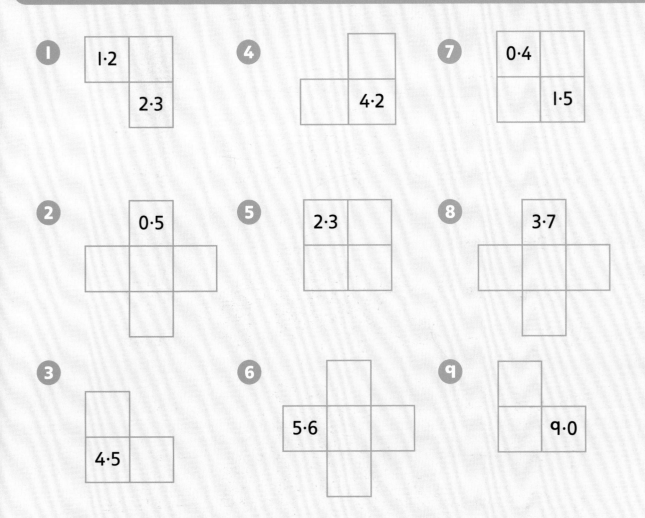

1. 1·2
    2·3

4. 4·2

7. 0·4
    1·5

2. 0·5

5. 2·3

8. 3·7

3. 4·5

6. 5·6

9. 9·0

● I am confident with placing decimal tenths on a
○ number square.
○

0·01	0·02	0·03	0·04	0·05
0·11	0·12	0·13	0·14	
0·21	0·22	0·23		
0·31	0·32			
0·41				

0·15
0·24 0·25

Copy and complete on squared paper.

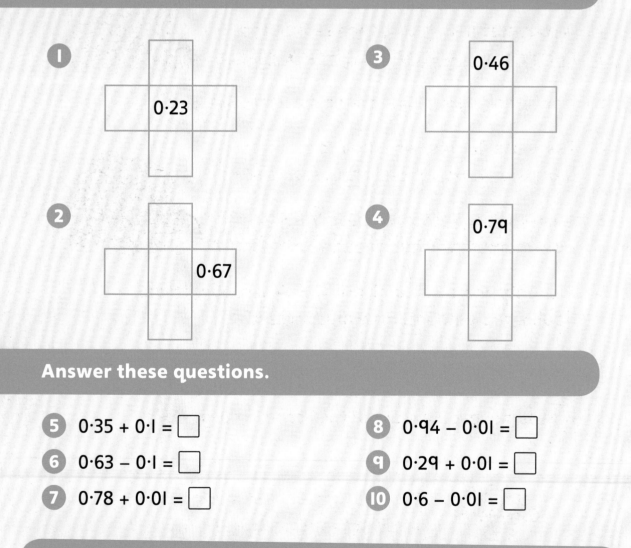

1 0·23

3 0·46

2 0·67

4 0·79

Answer these questions.

5 0·35 + 0·1 = ☐

6 0·63 – 0·1 = ☐

7 0·78 + 0·01 = ☐

8 0·94 – 0·01 = ☐

9 0·29 + 0·01 = ☐

10 0·6 – 0·01 = ☐

I am confident with placing decimal hundredths on a number square and can add and subtract tenths and hundredths.

Mental multiplication strategies

Solve these word problems.

1. For a school football tournament, 47 oranges are cut into quarters. How many quarters are there?

2. Filip cycled 28 km every day for 4 days. How far did he cycle?

3. A plant was 17 cm tall. In one month its height doubled. In the next month its height doubled again. How tall was it after two months?

4. A coat cost £118. It was then reduced to half price in a sale. What is its sale price?

5. How many horseshoes are needed for 38 horses?

6. There are 96 children who are split into groups of 4. How many groups are there?

7. A car-making factory has 256 wheels. How many cars is this enough for?

8. A charity was given a gift of £78. A second gift was double this amount. How much was it?

9. Half the number of people at a concert were adults and half of the adults were women. If there were 78 women, how many people were at the concert altogether?

 **THINK**   Make up three of your own doubling or halving word problems.

- I am confident with doubling and halving as a mental method of multiplication.

Multiply these numbers by 20.

It is easier to do these in two steps!

1 24   4 72   7 95

2 35   5 57   8 76

3 48   6 86   9 68

Multiply these numbers by 25.

10 32   13 62   16 85

11 16   14 34   17 72

12 52   15 56   18 66

Multiply these numbers by 9.

19 38   22 47   25 35

20 49   23 66   26 92

21 56   24 89   27 71

 **THINK** Would you prefer to use the grid method or the mental strategy you have been learning to multiply by 9? Explain why.

I am confident with using mental strategies to multiply by 20, 25 and 9.

Use mental strategies to answer these questions.

1 69 × 9 = ☐

2 48 × 25 = ☐

3 39 × 20 = ☐

4 81 × 9 = ☐

5 38 × 25 = ☐

6 86 × 20 = ☐

7 74 × 9 = ☐

8 67 × 25 = ☐

These are easier than they look!

9 77 × 20 = ☐

10 63 × 9 = ☐

11 91 × 25 = ☐

12 97 × 20 = ☐

13 72 × 9 = ☐

14 79 × 25 = ☐

15 89 × 20 = ☐

16 87 × 9 = ☐

Find the missing numbers.

17 69 × ☐ = 1725

18 71 × ☐ = 639

19 42 × ☐ = 1050

20 58 × ☐ = 522

THINK Write a method explaining to a Year 4 pupil how to multiply by 20 or 25. Explain why it works.

●
● **I am confident with using mental strategies to**
● **multiply by 20, 25 and 9.**

12- and 24-hour clock

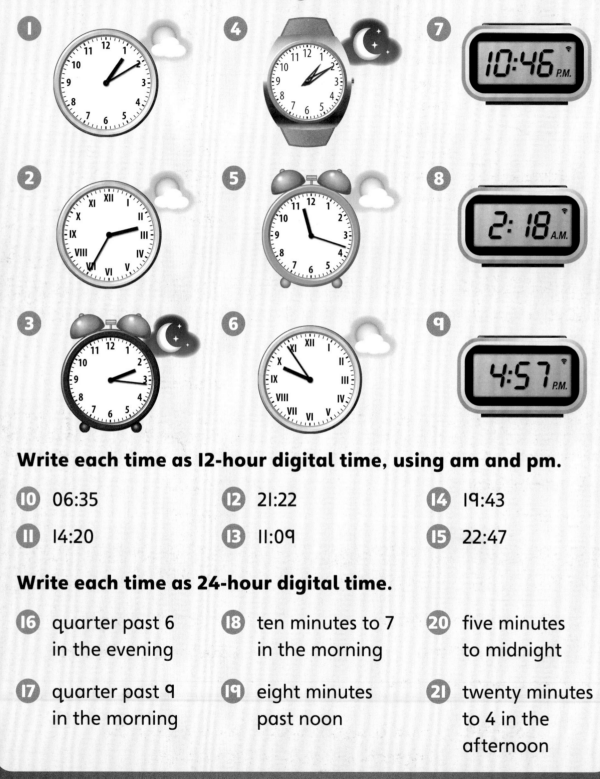

Write each time as 24-hour digital time.

1

4

7 10:46 P.M.

2

5

8 2:18 A.M.

3

6

9 4:57 P.M.

Write each time as 12-hour digital time, using am and pm.

10 06:35

11 14:20

12 21:22

13 11:09

14 19:43

15 22:47

Write each time as 24-hour digital time.

16 quarter past 6 in the evening

17 quarter past 9 in the morning

18 ten minutes to 7 in the morning

19 eight minutes past noon

20 five minutes to midnight

21 twenty minutes to 4 in the afternoon

I am confident with 12- and 24-hour clock times.

Read the timetable and answer the questions.

Place		Flight I	Flight 2	Flight 3
London	take off	10:30	12:30	14:30
Paris	land	11:35	13:35	15:35
	take off	12:05	14:05	16:05
Amsterdam	land	13:40	15:40	17:40
	take off	14:20	16:20	18:20
Dublin	land	15:55	17:55	19:55
	take off	16:25	18:25	20:25
Edinburgh	land	17:05	19:05	21:05
	take off	17:25	19:25	21:25
London	land	18:35	20:35	22:35

At what times do planes take off from:

1 Dublin?

2 London?

3 Paris?

4 Amsterdam?

At what times do planes land in:

5 Edinburgh?

6 Paris?

7 London?

8 Dublin?

How long are these journeys?

9 Amsterdam to Dublin

10 London to Paris

11 Edinburgh to London

12 Paris to Amsterdam

13 Dublin to Edinburgh

THINK How long does each plane stop at the airport between daytime flights?

I am confident with reading 24-hour times from a timetable and working out time intervals.

Dozetown
11:03
12:52
15:31
18:18

Sleepville
10:54
12:43
15:22
18:09

Snoreton
10:15
12:04
14:43
17:30

Little Boring
10:32
12:21
15:00
17:47

Snoozeford
11:26
13:15
15:54
18:41

Write how long it takes to get from:

2 Snoreton to Little Boring.

3 Sleepville to Dozetown.

4 Snoreton to Sleepville.

5 Sleepville to Snoozeford.

6 Little Boring to Sleepville.

7 Dozetown to Snoozeford.

8 Little Boring to Dozetown.

9 Little Boring to Snoozeford.

10 How long is the train's total journey?

THINK A train goes from A to B. It takes 2 hours and 45 minutes and stops in eight places. Create a timetable and calculate the time from each stop to the next.

I am confident with reading 24-hour times from a timetable and working out time intervals.

Length and perimeter

Measure each creature and write the length in millimetres and then in centimetres. Use the red dots to help you.

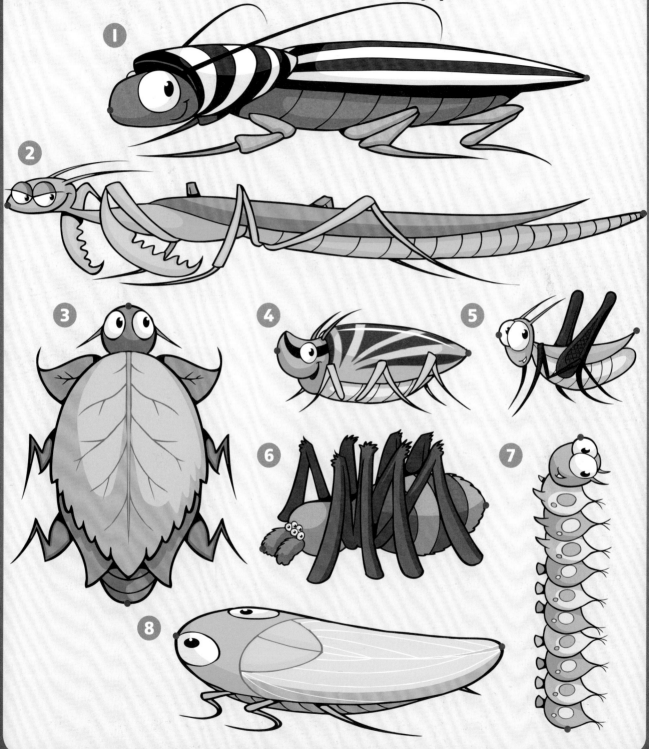

I am confident with measuring in centimetres and millimetres.

Measure each creature and write the length in millimetres and then in centimetres.

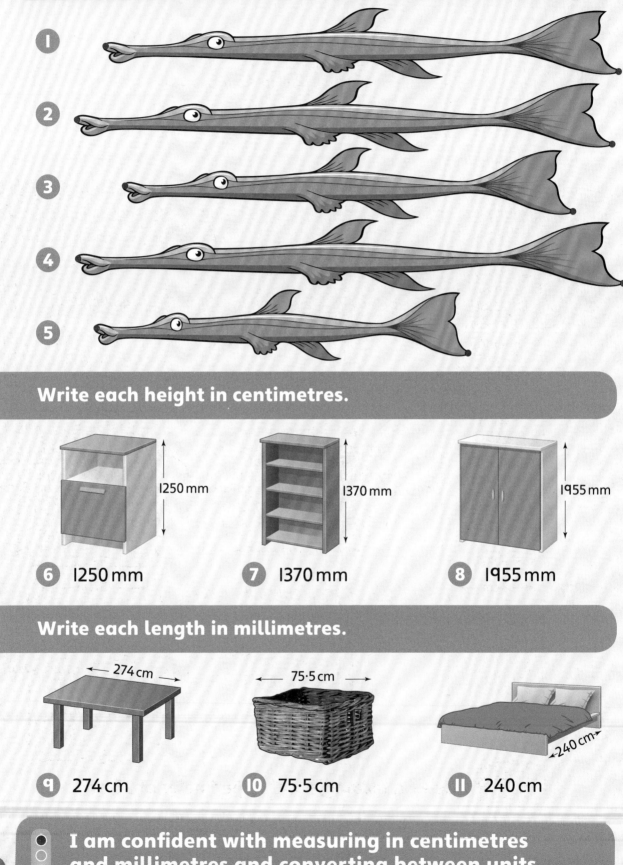

1

2

3

4

5

Write each height in centimetres.

1250 mm

1370 mm

1955 mm

6 1250 mm

7 1370 mm

8 1955 mm

Write each length in millimetres.

← 274 cm →

← 75·5 cm →

←240 cm→

9 274 cm

10 75·5 cm

11 240 cm

I am confident with measuring in centimetres and millimetres and converting between units.

Measure the perimeter of each rectangle in centimetres. Then write it in metres.

1

2

3

Calculate the perimeter of each photo and write it in centimetres and then in metres.

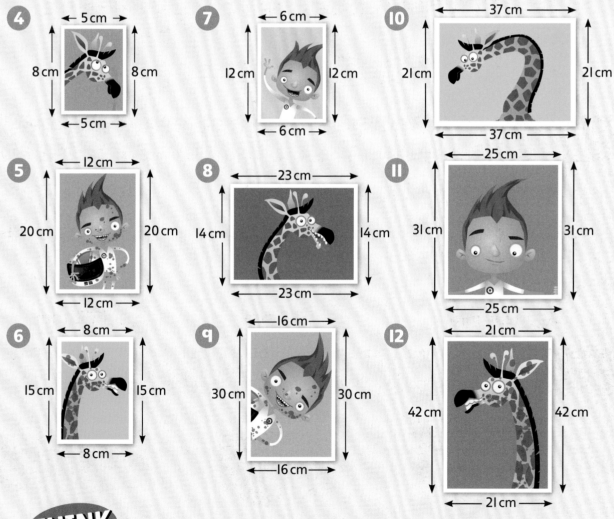

4 5 cm, 8 cm, 8 cm, 5 cm

5 12 cm, 20 cm, 20 cm, 12 cm

6 8 cm, 15 cm, 15 cm, 8 cm

7 6 cm, 12 cm, 12 cm, 6 cm

8 23 cm, 14 cm, 14 cm, 23 cm

9 16 cm, 30 cm, 30 cm, 16 cm

10 37 cm, 21 cm, 21 cm, 37 cm

11 25 cm, 31 cm, 31 cm, 25 cm

12 21 cm, 42 cm, 42 cm, 21 cm

THINK Draw a rectangle with a perimeter of 28 cm.

○ **I am confident with measuring and finding perimeters and converting centimetres into metres.**
○
○

Calculate the perimeter of each poster. Write your answer in metres.

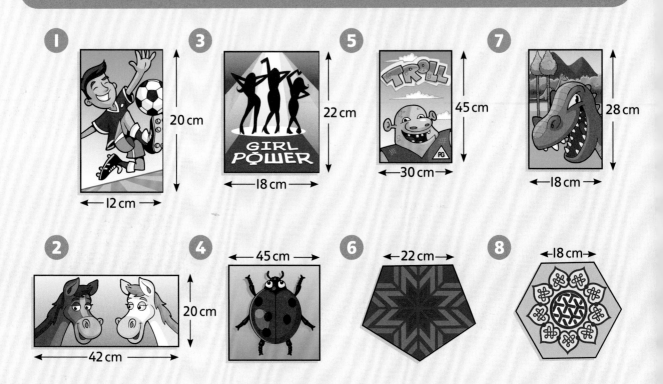

1 20 cm, 12 cm

3 22 cm, 18 cm

5 45 cm, 30 cm

7 28 cm, 18 cm

2 20 cm, 42 cm

4 45 cm, 20 cm

6 22 cm

8 18 cm

Write, in centimetres, the perimeter of the following.

9 A rectangle measuring 7 cm by 6 cm.

10 A rectangle measuring 6·5 cm by 3·5 cm.

11 A square with a side of 8 cm.

12 A square with a side of 4·25 cm.

13 An equilateral triangle with a side of 3·6 cm.

 The perimeter of a rectangle is 36 cm. Investigate what length sides the rectangle could have.

I am confident with finding perimeters and converting centimetres into metres.

**Write the perimeter of each shape in centimetres.
Then write it in metres.**

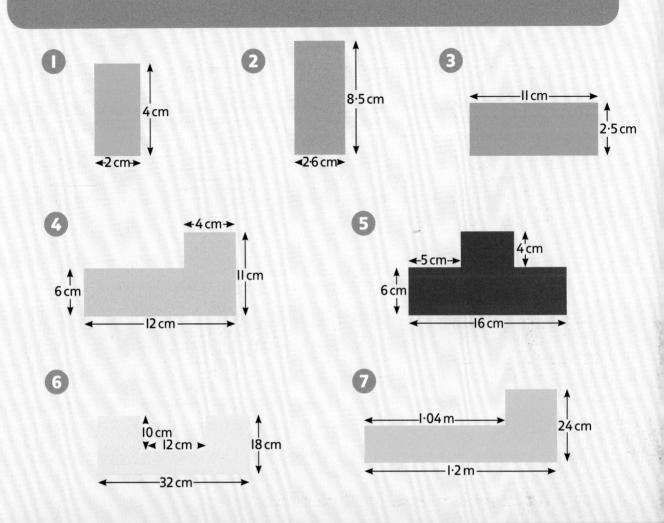

1. 4 cm, 2 cm
2. 8·5 cm, 2·6 cm
3. 11 cm, 2·5 cm
4. 4 cm, 11 cm, 6 cm, 12 cm
5. 5 cm, 4 cm, 6 cm, 16 cm
6. 10 cm, 12 cm, 18 cm, 32 cm
7. 1·04 m, 24 cm, 1·2 m

**Write the perimeter of these regular polygons
in centimetres and in metres.**

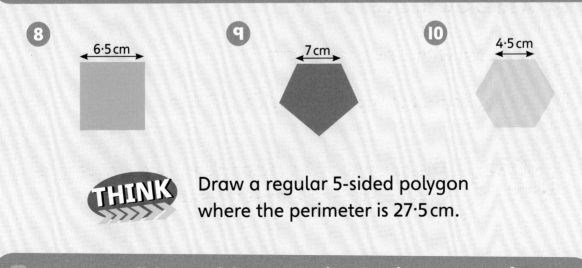

8. 6·5 cm
9. 7 cm
10. 4·5 cm

THINK Draw a regular 5-sided polygon
where the perimeter is 27·5 cm.

I am confident with measuring perimeters and
converting centimetres into metres.

Subtracting 3-digit numbers

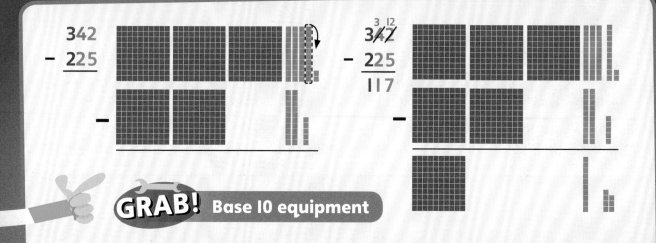

```
  342                              3 12
- 225                          3 4̸ 2̸
                              - 225
                              ─────
                                117
```

GRAB! Base 10 equipment

Use the method above for each subtraction.

1   384
     − 257

3   837
     − 343

5   415
     − 352

7   429
     − 356

2   452
     − 128

4   548
     − 293

6   381
     − 146

8   773
     − 657

> For some of these you will need to move a 100 as well.

9   932
     − 489

10   571
     − 385

11   942
     − 757

12   732
     − 688

○
○
○   **I am confident with subtracting 3-digit numbers using the column method.**

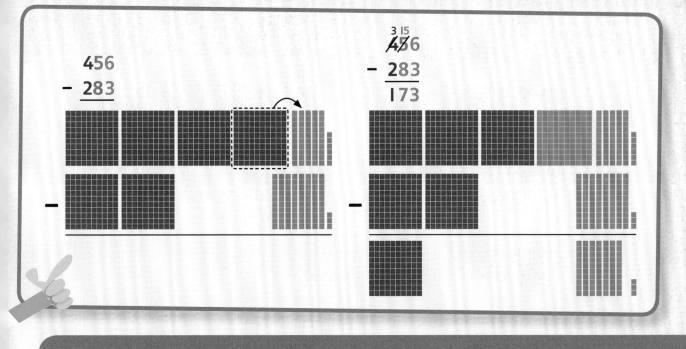

$$456 - 283$$

$$
\begin{array}{r}
\overset{3\ \ 15}{\cancel{4}\cancel{5}6} \\
-\ 283 \\
\hline
173
\end{array}
$$

Use the method above for each subtraction.

1   456
      − 283

2   937
      − 284

3   785
      − 467

4   947
      − 339

5   572
      − 468

6   559
      − 385

7   478
      − 294

8   617
      − 583

9   915
      − 662

10   405
      − 352

11   697
      − 448

12   780
      − 679

13   481
      − 356

14   866
      − 395

15   611
      − 306

16   942
      − 333

Rewrite these and answer them in the same way as above.

17 752 − 329 = ☐

18 486 − 291 = ☐

19 736 − 692 = ☐

20 814 − 352 = ☐

21 624 − 519 = ☐

22 949 − 494 = ☐

I am confident with subtracting 3-digit numbers using the column method.

39

Use the column method for each subtraction.

1   567
    − 283

3   971
    − 868

5   818
    − 662

7   591
    − 456

2   826
    − 395

4   448
    − 384

6   729
    − 652

8   876
    − 595

For each of these subtractions you will need to move two values across.

9   422
    − 283

10   516
     − 468

11   915
     − 668

12   431
     − 356

Solve these word problems.

13 The Empire State building is 443 m tall. The Eiffel Tower is 324 m tall. How much taller is the Empire State building?

14 The world's tallest man was 272 cm tall. How much taller was he than Sara, who is 169 cm tall?

15 678 people travelled on a ferry boat. At the first stop 392 got off. How many remained on the boat?

16 Feng has £365 in savings. He wants to buy a computer costing £573. How much more money does he need to save?

17 A block of cheese weighs 753 g. Dan cuts off a chunk weighing 247 g and eats it. How much cheese remains?

THINK   Write your own word problem for 476 subtract 348.

○ **I am confident with subtracting 3-digit numbers using the column method.**

Use the column method for each subtraction.

1 612 − 283

2 823 − 284

3 745 − 467

4 816 − 339

5 562 − 468

6 551 − 385

7 672 − 594

8 662 − 583

9 915 − 617

10 425 − 358

11 637 − 448

12 753 − 679

13 422 − 356

14 841 − 365

15 665 − 396

16 932 − 533

Solve these word problems.

17 The world's tallest man was 272 cm tall. How much taller was he than Ben, who is 195 cm tall?

18 In the year 2019 there are 365 days. On 7 July, 188 days of the year will have passed. How many days of the year will remain?

19 A cliff is 372 m tall. If a rope that is 286 m long is hung over the cliff, how far from the bottom of the cliff will it be?

 Write a subtraction that will give the answer 394 and that involves moving a hundred and a ten across.

I am confident with subtracting 3-digit numbers using the column method.

Use the column method for each subtraction. Check each answer with an addition.

(1) 645
   − 368

(2) 712
   − 293

(3) 617
   − 348

(4) 813
   − 685

(5) 671
   − 584

(6) 552
   − 464

(7) 972
   − 583

(8) 541
   − 386

(9) 837
   − 449

(10) 815
   − 737

(11) 552
   − 479

(12) 454
   − 358

(13) 565
   − 386

(14) 415
   − 356

(15) 732
   − 536

(16) 821
   − 365

Solve these word problems.

(17) Jim goes rock climbing. He climbs 468 m up a 624 m cliff face. How much further must he climb to reach the top?

(18) In the year 2016 there are 366 days. On 27 June, 179 days of the year will have passed. How many days of the year will remain?

THINK Find the missing numbers.

    7 3 4   6 5 3
  − ☐ ☐ ☐   − ☐ ☐ ☐
    2 5 2   2 2 7

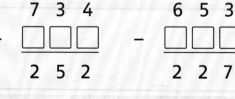

I am confident with subtracting 3-digit numbers using the column method.

42

Subtracting 3- and 4-digit numbers by counting up

Complete each subtraction by counting up.

1 803 – 657 = ☐

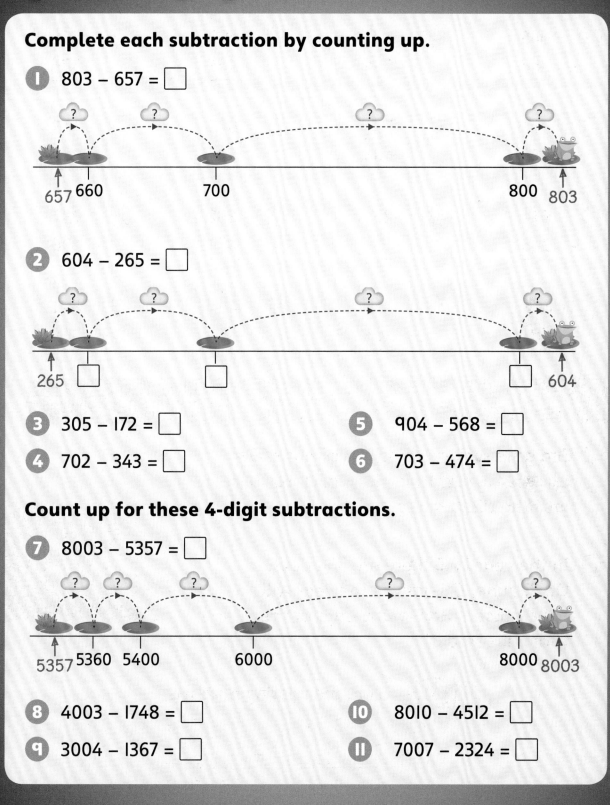

2 604 – 265 = ☐

3 305 – 172 = ☐   **5** 904 – 568 = ☐

4 702 – 343 = ☐   **6** 703 – 474 = ☐

Count up for these 4-digit subtractions.

7 8003 – 5357 = ☐

8 4003 – 1748 = ☐   **10** 8010 – 4512 = ☐

9 3004 – 1367 = ☐   **11** 7007 – 2324 = ☐

○
○ ○ **I am confident with subtracting 3- and 4-digit**
○ ○ **numbers using the mental method of counting up.**

43

1 Subtract one of the octopus numbers from one of the shark numbers. Do this six times.

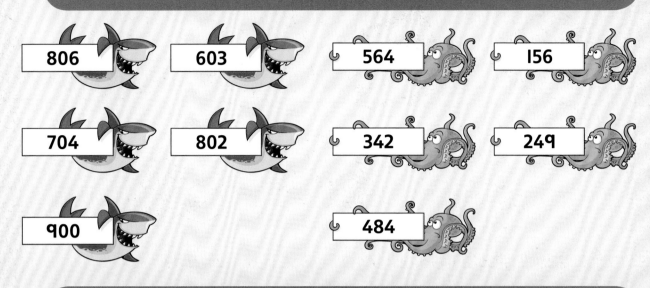

806   603   564   156

704   802   342   249

900   484

2 Subtract one of the octopus numbers from one of the shark numbers. Do this six times.

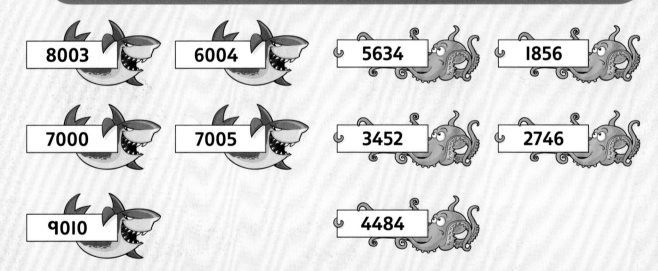

8003   6004   5634   1856

7000   7005   3452   2746

9010   4484

3 Choose four of your answers above to check using addition.

THINK

I'm thinking of a 4-digit number. I add 4782 to my number and get a 4-digit answer that is 8 greater than a multiple of 1000. What could my number be? Find at least three possible solutions.

I am confident with subtracting 3- and 4-digit numbers using the mental method of counting up.

Finding change by counting up

£7.99   £4.48   £48.36   £18.29

£17.90   £64.42   £30.78

1 Which single items above can you buy with £50?

2 How much change would you get from these items?

3 Are there two items that you could buy? If so, how much change would you get?

£78.98   £69.07   £61.22   £83.71

£93.70   £117   £52.89

4 Which of these seven single items can you buy with £100?

5 What change would you get?

THINK   Check two of your subtractions using addition.

○
○
○   **I am confident with subtracting money amounts to find change using the mental method of counting up.**

£13.70

£76.99

£8.29

£173.29

£39.66

£17.90

£33.48

£49.77

1. Choose two items that you can buy with £50. Find the change from £50. Do this three times.

2. Choose two items that you can buy with £100. Find the change from £100. Do this three times.

3. Choose two items that you can buy with £500. Find the change from £500. Do this three times.

4. Bolek buys some rock-climbing boots and a cycle helmet. How much change from £100 does he get?

5. Sam has £88. He buys a skateboard and a pair of shin pads. How much does he have after buying them?

6. Nisha buys two of the tennis rackets and is given an £18 discount. How much does she pay?

THINK Which three items above have a total that is closest to £100?

I am confident with subtracting money amounts to find change using the mental method of counting up.

Multiples and factors

The animals are going to the wildlife park. Can they be paired exactly in 2s? Write yes or no for each animal.

1. 47 giraffes
2. 138 lions
3. 427 llamas
4. 245 kangaroos
5. 97 rhinos

6. 56 horses
7. 249 tigers
8. 109 monkeys
9. 1008 buffalo
10. 164 hippos

11. 84 zebras
12. 54 elephants
13. 386 emus
14. 478 snakes
15. 300 ostriches

The bank has bags of coins of the same type. For each bag write whether they could contain all 2p coins, all 5p coins or all 10p coins.

16. COINS 70p
17. COINS 85p
18. COINS 90p
19. COINS 64p

20. COINS 96p
21. COINS £3·20
22. COINS £4·50
23. COINS £1·75

24. COINS £2·33
25. COINS £3·15
26. COINS £4·28
27. COINS £5·36

I am confident with identifying multiples of 2, 5 and 10.

Leap years are divisible by 4. Which of these are leap years? Write yes or no for each year.

1 2008

2 1394

3 1994

4 1942

5 4048

6 1708

7 866

8 1582

9 2024

10 1275

11 1943

12 2070

13 **Copy and complete this table.**

Number	Divisible by:			
	2	5	9	4
76	✔	✗	✗	✔
85				
142				
2136				
3024				
8005				
790				
4122				

THINK A test for divisibility by 4 is to halve the number and see if the result is an even number.
Can you create a similar test for divisibility by 8? Show how this test works giving numbers that are and are not divisible by 8.

I am confident with identifying multiples of 2, 4, 5 and 9.

Find different factor pairs for these numbers.

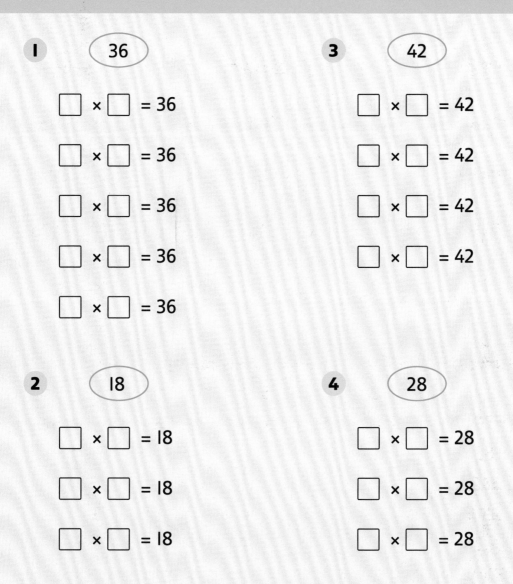

1 (36)

☐ × ☐ = 36

☐ × ☐ = 36

☐ × ☐ = 36

☐ × ☐ = 36

☐ × ☐ = 36

3 (42)

☐ × ☐ = 42

☐ × ☐ = 42

☐ × ☐ = 42

☐ × ☐ = 42

2 (18)

☐ × ☐ = 18

☐ × ☐ = 18

☐ × ☐ = 18

4 (28)

☐ × ☐ = 28

☐ × ☐ = 28

☐ × ☐ = 28

5 There are 48 guests at a party. They need to be arranged at tables. How many tables will you need and how many guests will sit at each table? Find as many different ways as you can to do this.

6 When the length and the width of a rectangle are multiplied together, the answer (the area) is 30 cm². Find different possible lengths and widths for this rectangle.

● I am confident with finding factor pairs for a given
○
○ number.
○

Comparing fractions and finding equivalents

$\frac{2}{6} < \frac{3}{8}$

I whole									
$\frac{1}{2}$					$\frac{1}{2}$				
$\frac{1}{3}$			$\frac{1}{3}$			$\frac{1}{3}$			
$\frac{1}{4}$		$\frac{1}{4}$		$\frac{1}{4}$			$\frac{1}{4}$		
$\frac{1}{5}$		$\frac{1}{5}$		$\frac{1}{5}$		$\frac{1}{5}$		$\frac{1}{5}$	
$\frac{1}{6}$	$\frac{1}{6}$		$\frac{1}{6}$		$\frac{1}{6}$		$\frac{1}{6}$		$\frac{1}{6}$
$\frac{1}{7}$	$\frac{1}{7}$	$\frac{1}{7}$		$\frac{1}{7}$	$\frac{1}{7}$		$\frac{1}{7}$		$\frac{1}{7}$
$\frac{1}{8}$	$\frac{1}{8}$	$\frac{1}{8}$	$\frac{1}{8}$		$\frac{1}{8}$	$\frac{1}{8}$	$\frac{1}{8}$		$\frac{1}{8}$
$\frac{1}{9}$	$\frac{1}{9}$	$\frac{1}{9}$	$\frac{1}{9}$	$\frac{1}{9}$		$\frac{1}{9}$	$\frac{1}{9}$	$\frac{1}{9}$	$\frac{1}{9}$
$\frac{1}{10}$	$\frac{1}{10}$	$\frac{1}{10}$	$\frac{1}{10}$	$\frac{1}{10}$	$\frac{1}{10}$	$\frac{1}{10}$	$\frac{1}{10}$	$\frac{1}{10}$	$\frac{1}{10}$

Compare each pair of fractions. Write > or < between them.

1. $\frac{3}{6}$ $\frac{4}{9}$

2. $\frac{2}{3}$ $\frac{7}{8}$

3. $\frac{3}{4}$ $\frac{4}{5}$

4. $\frac{3}{10}$ $\frac{2}{9}$

5. $\frac{5}{8}$ $\frac{4}{6}$

6. $\frac{4}{6}$ $\frac{7}{9}$

7. $\frac{5}{8}$ $\frac{6}{10}$

8. $\frac{2}{3}$ $\frac{4}{5}$

9. $\frac{2}{5}$ $\frac{3}{8}$

10. $\frac{2}{8}$ $\frac{2}{9}$

11. $\frac{5}{6}$ $\frac{4}{5}$

12. $\frac{6}{10}$ $\frac{5}{8}$

13. $\frac{2}{3}$ $\frac{6}{7}$

14. $\frac{7}{8}$ $\frac{8}{9}$

15. $\frac{2}{7}$ $\frac{3}{10}$

THINK   Write four fractions which are greater than a half and four that are less than a half. Then write two fractions that are equal to a half.

I am confident with comparing non-unit fractions.

Use the number lines to help you write < or > between each pair of fractions.

0 ├──┼──┼──┼──┼──┼──┼──┼──┼──┼──┼──┼──┼──┤ 1

1 $\frac{1}{2}$ $\frac{7}{12}$

3 $\frac{3}{4}$ $\frac{11}{12}$

2 $\frac{5}{6}$ $\frac{2}{3}$

4 $\frac{1}{3}$ $\frac{1}{4}$

0 ├──┼──┼──┼──┼──┼──┼──┼──┼──┼──┼──┼──┼──┼──┼──┼──┤ 1

5 $\frac{4}{5}$ $\frac{9}{10}$

7 $\frac{3}{4}$ $\frac{4}{5}$

6 $\frac{13}{20}$ $\frac{3}{5}$

8 $\frac{1}{4}$ $\frac{9}{20}$

Write > or < between each pair of fractions.

9 $\frac{5}{8}$ $\frac{1}{2}$

11 $\frac{4}{5}$ $\frac{18}{20}$

13 $\frac{3}{8}$ $\frac{1}{4}$

10 $\frac{6}{15}$ $\frac{1}{3}$

12 $\frac{1}{2}$ $\frac{7}{16}$

14 $\frac{7}{15}$ $\frac{13}{30}$

Draw a number line split into 16 equal parts. Mark these fractions on it.

15 $\frac{1}{16}$

17 $\frac{3}{8}$

19 $\frac{7}{8}$

21 $\frac{1}{4}$

16 $\frac{1}{2}$

18 $\frac{3}{4}$

20 $\frac{15}{16}$

22 $\frac{5}{8}$

THINK Draw two number lines, one marked in 10ths and one marked in 12ths. With a partner choose a number line each. Choose a fraction each on your number line and compare them. Write them in order using < or =. Do this four times.

● I am confident with comparing fractions.
○
○

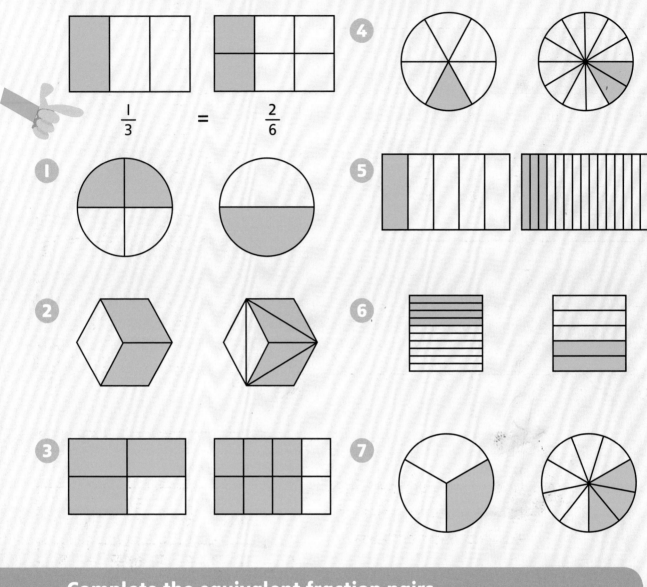

$\dfrac{1}{3}$ = $\dfrac{2}{6}$

Complete the equivalent fraction pairs.

8 $\dfrac{3}{4} = \dfrac{\square}{8}$

9 $\dfrac{\square}{4} = \dfrac{2}{8}$

10 $\dfrac{1}{5} = \dfrac{\square}{10}$

11 $\dfrac{4}{\square} = \dfrac{8}{10}$

12 $\dfrac{4}{8} = \dfrac{\square}{6}$

13 $\dfrac{4}{6} = \dfrac{\square}{3}$

⬤ **I am confident with recognising equivalent fractions.**
◯
◯

Copy and complete. Use the number lines to help you.

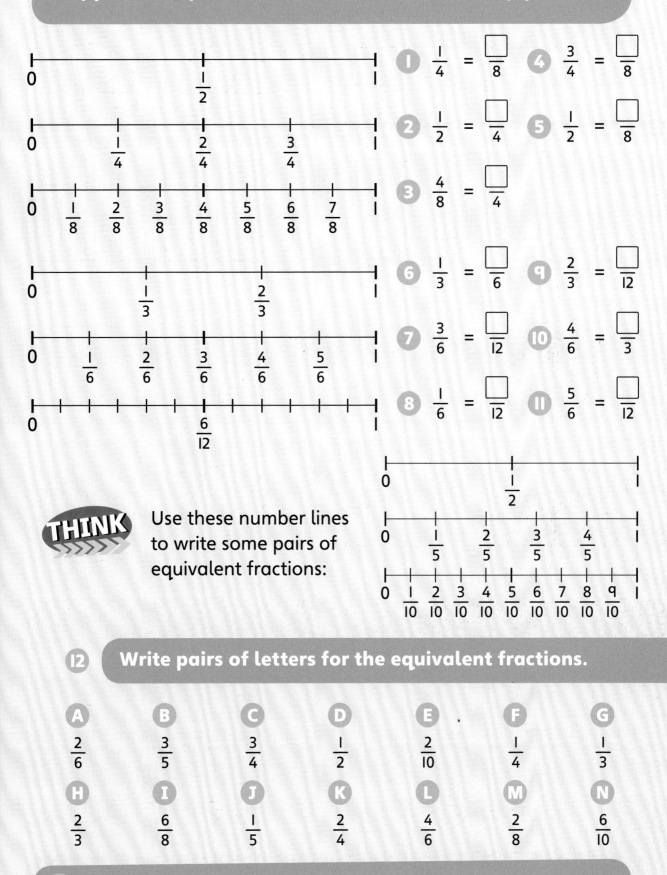

1. $\dfrac{1}{4} = \dfrac{\square}{8}$ 4. $\dfrac{3}{4} = \dfrac{\square}{8}$

2. $\dfrac{1}{2} = \dfrac{\square}{4}$ 5. $\dfrac{1}{2} = \dfrac{\square}{8}$

3. $\dfrac{4}{8} = \dfrac{\square}{4}$

6. $\dfrac{1}{3} = \dfrac{\square}{6}$ 9. $\dfrac{2}{3} = \dfrac{\square}{12}$

7. $\dfrac{3}{6} = \dfrac{\square}{12}$ 10. $\dfrac{4}{6} = \dfrac{\square}{3}$

8. $\dfrac{1}{6} = \dfrac{\square}{12}$ 11. $\dfrac{5}{6} = \dfrac{\square}{12}$

THINK Use these number lines to write some pairs of equivalent fractions:

12. **Write pairs of letters for the equivalent fractions.**

A $\dfrac{2}{6}$ B $\dfrac{3}{5}$ C $\dfrac{3}{4}$ D $\dfrac{1}{2}$ E $\dfrac{2}{10}$ F $\dfrac{1}{4}$ G $\dfrac{1}{3}$

H $\dfrac{2}{3}$ I $\dfrac{6}{8}$ J $\dfrac{1}{5}$ K $\dfrac{2}{4}$ L $\dfrac{4}{6}$ M $\dfrac{2}{8}$ N $\dfrac{6}{10}$

I am confident with finding equivalent fractions and simplifying fractions.

53

Write the fraction indicated by each letter and an equivalent fraction for it.

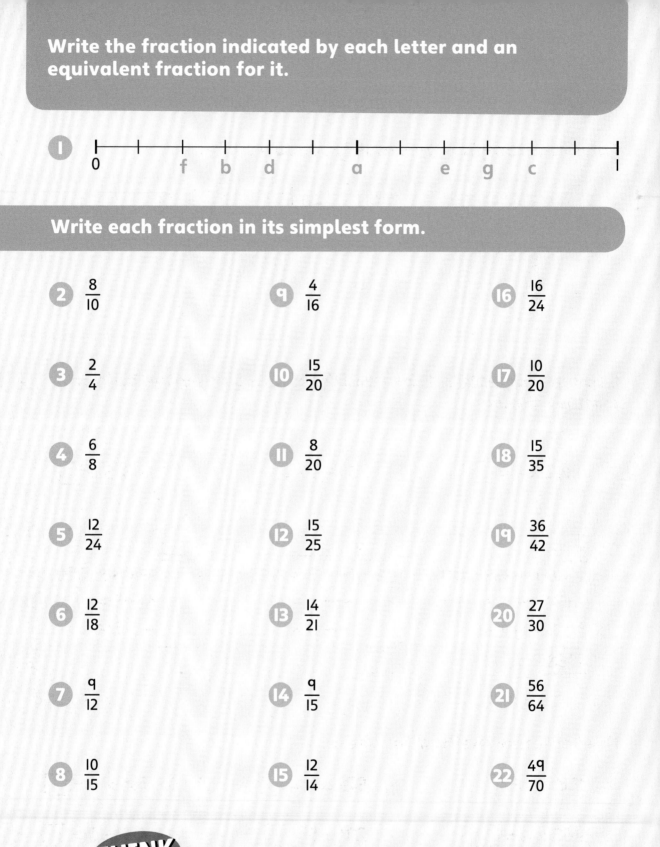

1

0   f   b   d   a   e   g   c   1

Write each fraction in its simplest form.

2 $\frac{8}{10}$

3 $\frac{2}{4}$

4 $\frac{6}{8}$

5 $\frac{12}{24}$

6 $\frac{12}{18}$

7 $\frac{9}{12}$

8 $\frac{10}{15}$

9 $\frac{4}{16}$

10 $\frac{15}{20}$

11 $\frac{8}{20}$

12 $\frac{15}{25}$

13 $\frac{14}{21}$

14 $\frac{9}{15}$

15 $\frac{12}{14}$

16 $\frac{16}{24}$

17 $\frac{10}{20}$

18 $\frac{15}{35}$

19 $\frac{36}{42}$

20 $\frac{27}{30}$

21 $\frac{56}{64}$

22 $\frac{49}{70}$

THINK   Write four fractions which simplify to $\frac{2}{3}$.

I am confident with finding equivalent fractions and simplifying fractions.

Multiplying 3- and 4-digit numbers by 1-digit numbers

Copy and complete this multiplication table.

I

×	60	300	40	200	90	700
5						
4						
3						
6						

Copy and complete these multiplications using the ladder method shown.

$342 \times 4 = \square$

```
   342
 ×   4
  1200 ←—— 4 × 300
   160 ←—— 4 ×  40
 +   8 ←—— 4 ×   2
  ————
  1368
```

2 $524 \times 3 = \square$

```
   524
 ×   3
       ←—— 3 × 500
       ←—— 3 ×  20
       ←—— 3 ×   4
  ————
```

3 $294 \times 5 = \square$

```
   294
 ×   5
       ←—— 5 × 200
       ←—— 5 ×
       ←—— 5 ×
  ————
```

Use the same method for these.

4 $158 \times 3 = \square$ **6** $927 \times 3 = \square$ **8** $785 \times 4 = \square$

5 $468 \times 4 = \square$ **7** $291 \times 5 = \square$ **9** $369 \times 5 = \square$

⦿ **I am confident with multiplying 3-digit numbers by 1-digit numbers using the ladder method.**

55

Use the ladder method for each multiplication.

353 × 4 = ☐

353
× 4

1200 ←— 4 × 300
200 ←— 4 × 50
+ 12 ←— 4 × 3

1412

6 2574 × 3 = ☐

2574
× 3

6000 ←— 3 × 2000
1500 ←— 3 × 500
210 ←— 3 × 70
+ 12 ←— 3 × 4

------

1 553 × 3 = ☐

2 784 × 4 = ☐

3 667 × 5 = ☐

4 194 × 3 = ☐

5 687 × 4 = ☐

7 1645 × 4 = ☐

8 4552 × 3 = ☐

9 3467 × 5 = ☐

10 6864 × 4 = ☐

11 3735 × 3 = ☐

Find the cost of these holidays for a) 3 people b) 4 people and c) 5 people.

12 GREECE
£318 each

13 PORTUGAL
£274 each

14 TUNISIA
£437 each

● I am confident with multiplying 3- and 4-digit numbers
○ by 1-digit numbers using the ladder method.
○

Use the ladder method to do these multiplications.

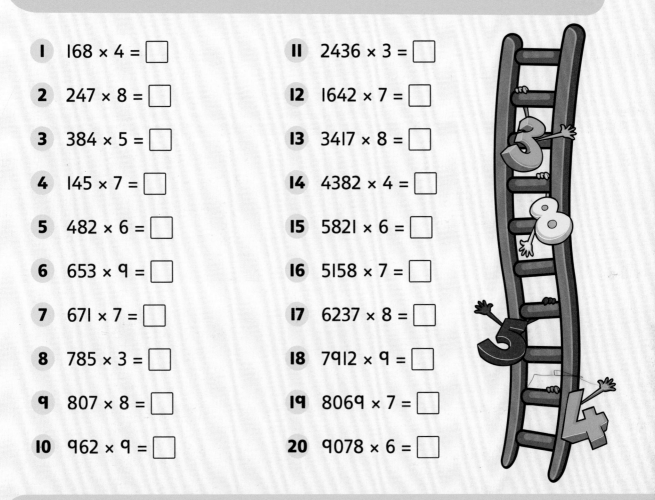

1. 168 × 4 = ☐
2. 247 × 8 = ☐
3. 384 × 5 = ☐
4. 145 × 7 = ☐
5. 482 × 6 = ☐
6. 653 × 9 = ☐
7. 671 × 7 = ☐
8. 785 × 3 = ☐
9. 807 × 8 = ☐
10. 962 × 9 = ☐

11. 2436 × 3 = ☐
12. 1642 × 7 = ☐
13. 3417 × 8 = ☐
14. 4382 × 4 = ☐
15. 5821 × 6 = ☐
16. 5158 × 7 = ☐
17. 6237 × 8 = ☐
18. 7912 × 9 = ☐
19. 8069 × 7 = ☐
20. 9078 × 6 = ☐

Solve these word problems.

21. A shop sells TVs that cost £586 each.
In one week they sell 6 of them.
How much money do they get?

GREAT OFFERS! TVs £586

22. A plane flies 486 miles every day.
How far does it fly in one week?

23. It is 1437 m from Leon's house to his office. How far does he walk in 4 days if he walks there and back each day?

- ● I am confident with multiplying 3- and 4-digit numbers
- ● by 1-digit numbers using the ladder method.
- ●

57

**Estimate the answer to these multiplications.
Then use the ladder method to work them out.**

1   358 × 4 = ☐

2   8 × 644 = ☐

3   643
    ×   7
    ‾‾‾‾‾

4   6 × 2438

5   978 × 4 = ☐

6   3821
    ×   8
    ‾‾‾‾‾

7   6 × 9856

8   3609 × 4 = ☐

9   586
    ×   8
    ‾‾‾‾‾

10   7 × 789

11   8472 × 3 = ☐

12   7 × 7859 = ☐

13   9527
     ×   8
     ‾‾‾‾‾

14   946 × 6 = ☐

15   9607
     ×   4
     ‾‾‾‾‾

16   6835 × 8 = ☐

17   859 × 9 = ☐

18   4653 × 7 = ☐

19   788
     ×   6
     ‾‾‾‾‾

20   4786 × 8 = ☐

THINK   A number, when it is divided by 4, has the answer 364. What is the number? Write two more puzzles like this for a partner to solve.

I am confident with multiplying 3- and 4-digit numbers by 1-digit numbers using the ladder method.

Try to find multiplications for each target answer using one number from each set. Use the ladder method. Make estimates first.

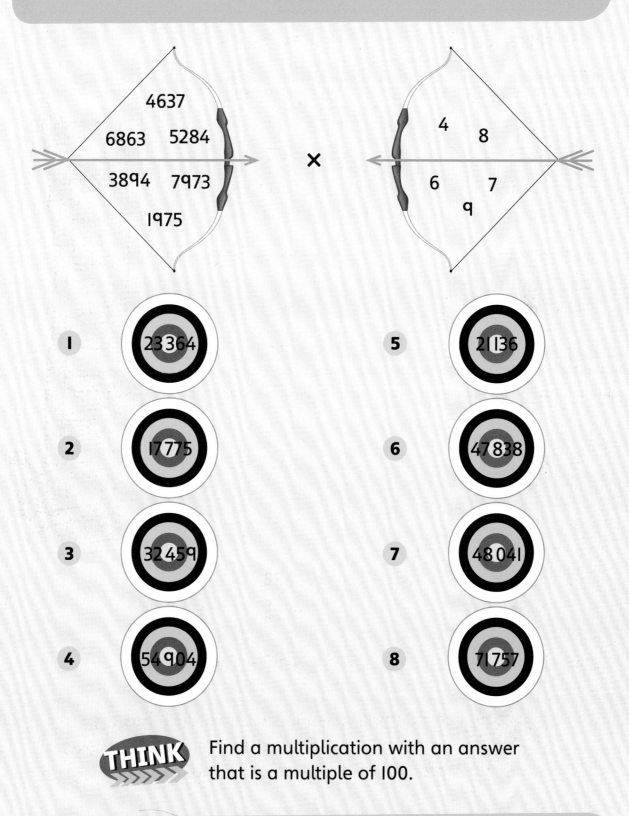

4637

6863   5284

3894   7973

1975

×

4   8

6   7

9

1 23 364

2 17 775

3 32 459

4 54 904

5 21 136

6 47 838

7 48 041

8 71 757

THINK Find a multiplication with an answer that is a multiple of 100.

●
● **I am confident with multiplying 4-digit numbers by**
● **1-digit numbers using the ladder method.**

Dividing 3-digit numbers by 1-digit numbers

10 × 4 = 40
20 × 4 = 80
30 × 4 = 120

114 ÷ 4 = ☐

☐ × 4 = 114
20 × 4 = 80
                    34
8 × 4 = 32
                    2
28

114 ÷ 4 = 28 r 2

1 × 4 =   4
2 × 4 =   8
3 × 4 = 12
4 × 4 = 16
5 × 4 = 20
6 × 4 = 24
7 × 4 = 28
8 × 4 = 32
9 × 4 = 36

Use similar jottings to do these divisions.

1   116 ÷ 5 = ☐

10 × 5 = 50
20 × 5 = 100
30 × 5 = 150

1 × 5 =   5
2 × 5 = 10
3 × 5 = 15
4 × 5 = 20
5 × 5 = 25
6 × 5 = 30
7 × 5 = 35
8 × 5 = 40
9 × 5 = 45

2   137 ÷ 4 = ☐   **8**   145 ÷ 4 = ☐

3   148 ÷ 5 = ☐   **9**   193 ÷ 5 = ☐

4   198 ÷ 9 = ☐   **10**   252 ÷ 9 = ☐

5   109 ÷ 4 = ☐   **11**   115 ÷ 3 = ☐

6   236 ÷ 9 = ☐   **12**   149 ÷ 6 = ☐

7   108 ÷ 3 = ☐   **13**   219 ÷ 8 = ☐

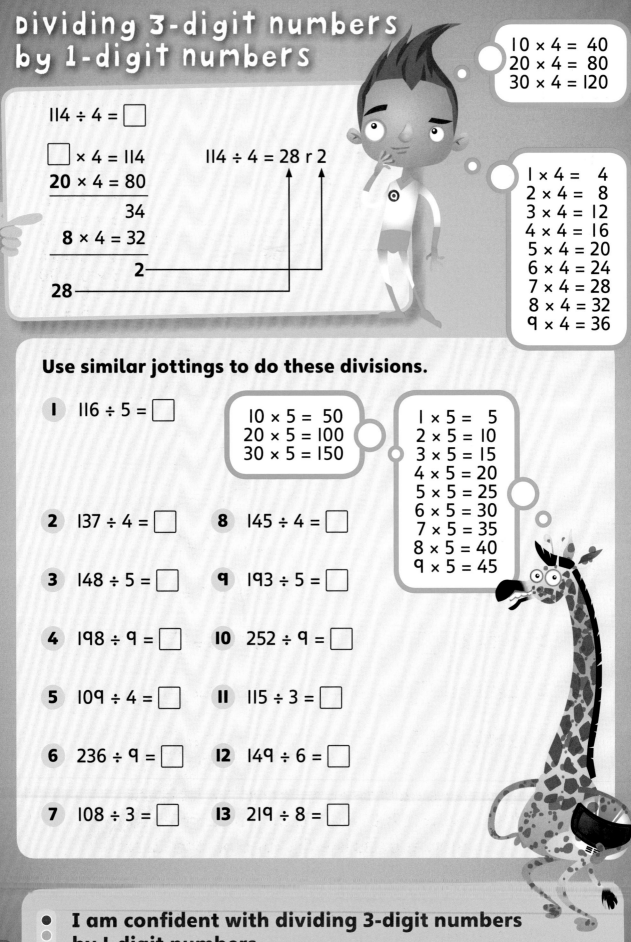

● **I am confident with dividing 3-digit numbers by 1-digit numbers.**
○
○

Answer these divisions.

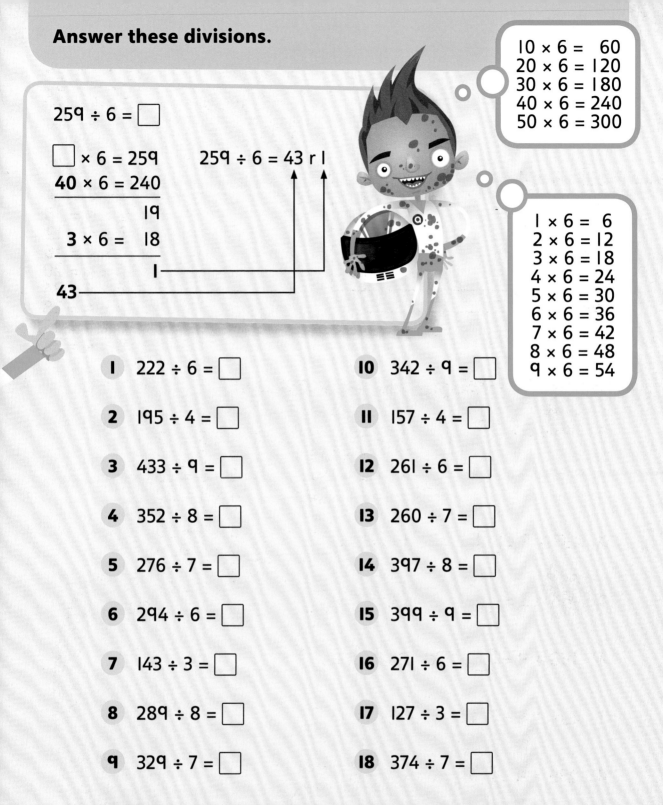

$10 \times 6 = 60$
$20 \times 6 = 120$
$30 \times 6 = 180$
$40 \times 6 = 240$
$50 \times 6 = 300$

$259 \div 6 = \square$

$\square \times 6 = 259$ $259 \div 6 = 43 \text{ r } 1$
$40 \times 6 = 240$
                    19
$\underline{3 \times 6 = 18}$
                    1
43

$1 \times 6 = 6$
$2 \times 6 = 12$
$3 \times 6 = 18$
$4 \times 6 = 24$
$5 \times 6 = 30$
$6 \times 6 = 36$
$7 \times 6 = 42$
$8 \times 6 = 48$
$9 \times 6 = 54$

1   $222 \div 6 = \square$

2   $195 \div 4 = \square$

3   $433 \div 9 = \square$

4   $352 \div 8 = \square$

5   $276 \div 7 = \square$

6   $294 \div 6 = \square$

7   $143 \div 3 = \square$

8   $289 \div 8 = \square$

9   $329 \div 7 = \square$

10   $342 \div 9 = \square$

11   $157 \div 4 = \square$

12   $261 \div 6 = \square$

13   $260 \div 7 = \square$

14   $397 \div 8 = \square$

15   $399 \div 9 = \square$

16   $271 \div 6 = \square$

17   $127 \div 3 = \square$

18   $374 \div 7 = \square$

 A number, when multiplied by 7, has the answer 266. What is the number? Write two more puzzles like this for a partner to solve.

- **I am confident with dividing 3-digit numbers by 1-digit numbers.**

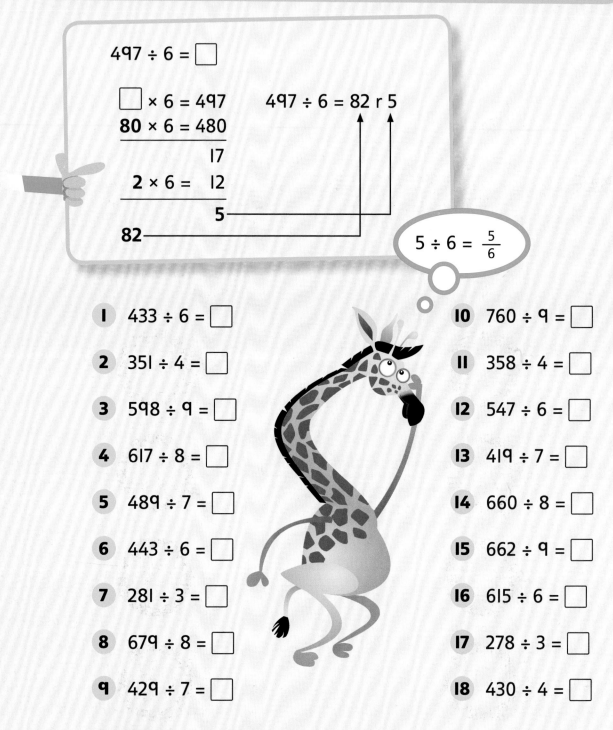

$497 \div 6 = \square$

$\square \times 6 = 497$ $497 \div 6 = 82 \text{ r } 5$

$80 \times 6 = 480$

17

$2 \times 6 = 12$

5

82

$5 \div 6 = \dfrac{5}{6}$

1 $433 \div 6 = \square$

2 $351 \div 4 = \square$

3 $598 \div 9 = \square$

4 $617 \div 8 = \square$

5 $489 \div 7 = \square$

6 $443 \div 6 = \square$

7 $281 \div 3 = \square$

8 $679 \div 8 = \square$

9 $429 \div 7 = \square$

10 $760 \div 9 = \square$

11 $358 \div 4 = \square$

12 $547 \div 6 = \square$

13 $419 \div 7 = \square$

14 $660 \div 8 = \square$

15 $662 \div 9 = \square$

16 $615 \div 6 = \square$

17 $278 \div 3 = \square$

18 $430 \div 4 = \square$

THINK A 3-digit number is divided by a 1-digit number. The answer is $67\frac{1}{2}$. What could the numbers be? Find at least three possible solutions.

I am confident with dividing 3-digit numbers by 1-digit numbers and expressing the remainder as a fraction.

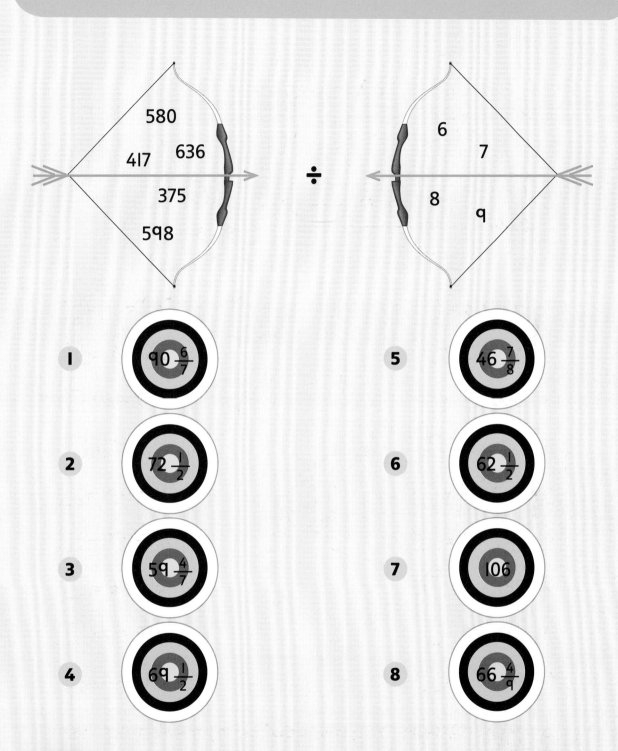

580
417   636
375
598

÷

6
7
8
9

1   $90\frac{6}{7}$

2   $72\frac{1}{2}$

3   $59\frac{4}{7}$

4   $69\frac{1}{2}$

5   $46\frac{7}{8}$

6   $62\frac{1}{2}$

7   106

8   $66\frac{4}{9}$

THINK   Find the division that has the answer closest to 100 and give its correct answer, with the remainder as a fraction.

● I am confident with dividing 3-digit numbers by 1-digit
○ numbers and expressing the remainder as a fraction.

63

Measuring angles

Estimate the size of each angle. Then use a protractor to measure it. Say whether each angle is acute or obtuse.

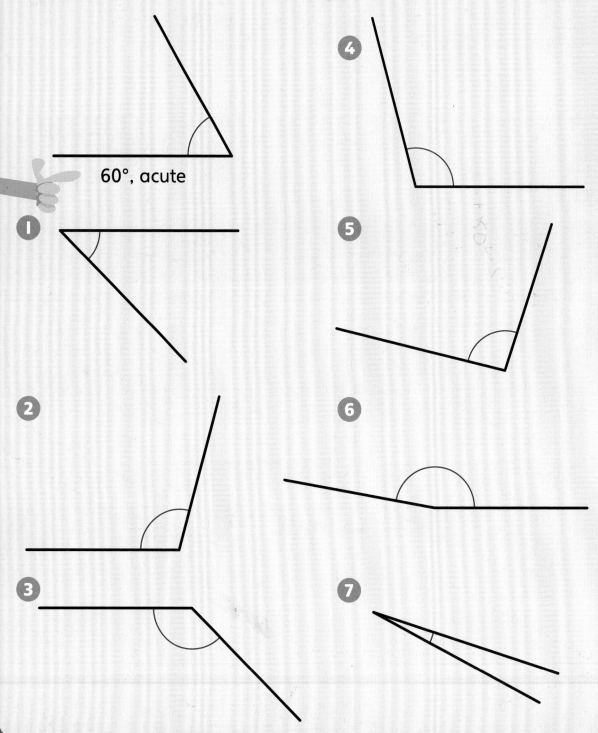

60°, acute

1

2

3

4

5

6

7

○ **I am confident with measuring angles and**
○
○ **recognising whether they are acute or obtuse.**

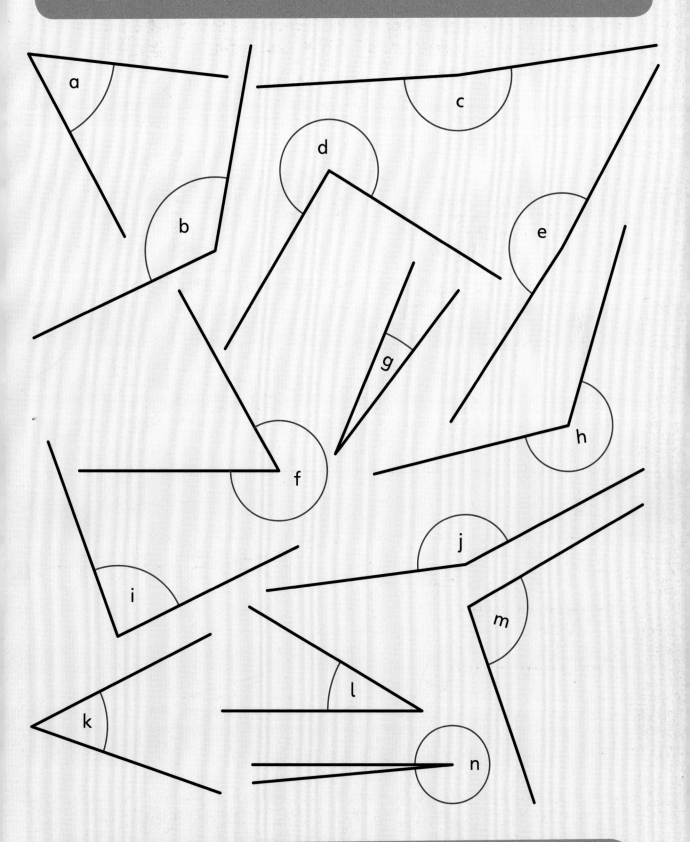

Estimate the size of each angle in each shape. Then measure them. Decide whether each angle is acute, obtuse or reflex.

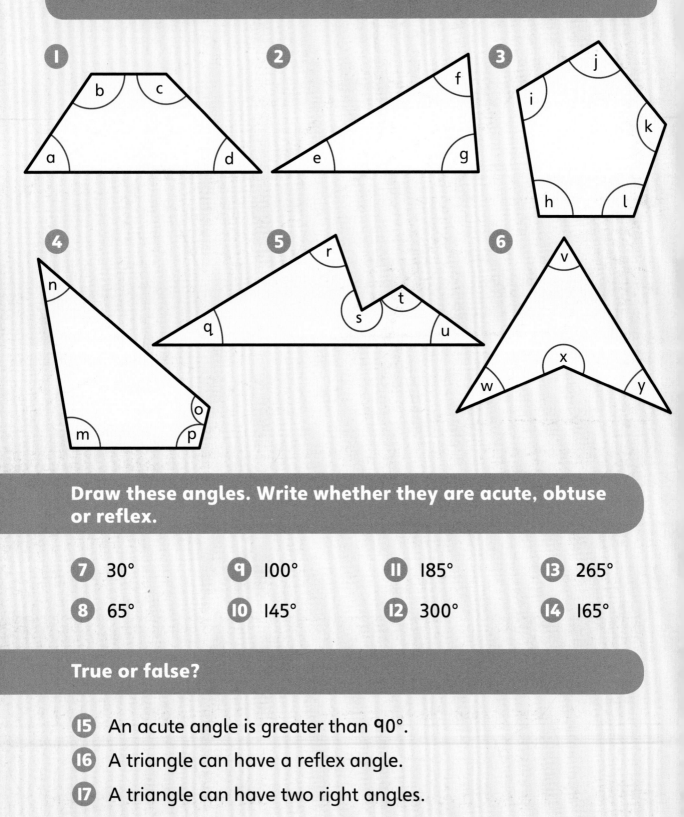

Draw these angles. Write whether they are acute, obtuse or reflex.

7 30° **9** 100° **11** 185° **13** 265°

8 65° **10** 145° **12** 300° **14** 165°

True or false?

15 An acute angle is greater than 90°.

16 A triangle can have a reflex angle.

17 A triangle can have two right angles.

I am confident with measuring and drawing angles, and recognising whether they are acute, obtuse or reflex.

Estimate the size of each angle in each shape. Then measure them. Decide whether each angle is acute, obtuse or reflex.

1 b c a d

2 f e

3 j k i h l g

4 n q o m p r s t u

5

6 v x w y

Draw these angles. Write whether they are acute, obtuse or reflex.

7 47°

8 89°

9 106°

10 173°

11 192°

12 264°

13 347°

14 93°

Draw a shape with as many reflex angles as you can. Measure the angles and copy and complete the table.

15

Number of sides	Number of reflex angles	Measure of reflex angles

THINK A quadrilateral could have two reflex angles. True or false?

○ **I am confident with measuring and drawing angles, and recognising whether they are acute, obtuse or reflex.**

Find the size of the angle marked with a letter.

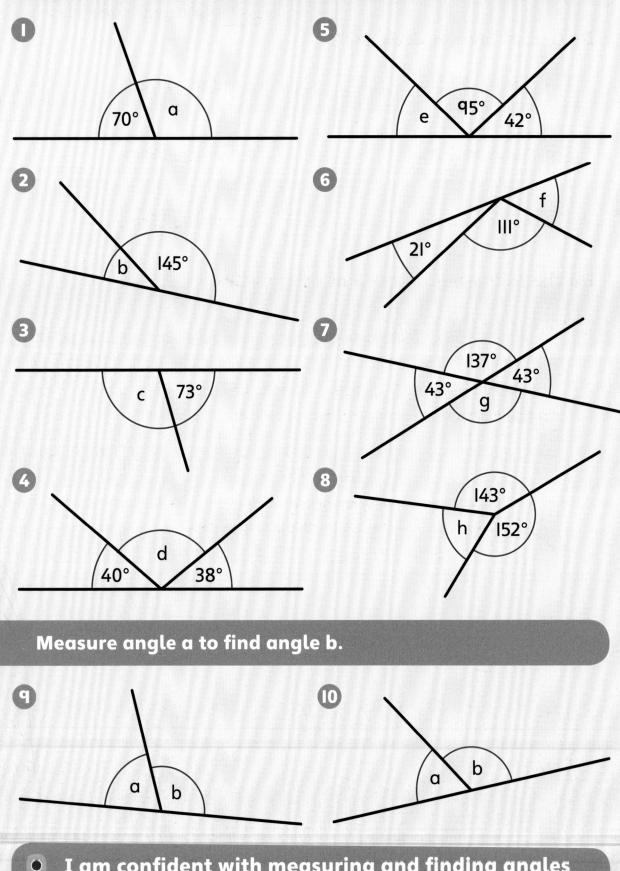

1. 70° a

5. 95° e 42°

2. b 145°

6. 21° 111° f

3. c 73°

7. 137° 43° 43° g

4. d 40° 38°

8. 143° h 152°

Measure angle a to find angle b.

9. a b

10. a b

● ○ ○ ○ I am confident with measuring and finding angles on a line and around a point.

circles

Draw and label a circle with:

1 a radius of 7 cm.

4 a radius of 8 cm.

2 a radius of 3 cm.

5 a radius of 6 cm.

3 a radius of 4 cm.

6 a radius of 5 cm.

Do the following for each of your circles.

7 Write the diameter.

8 Measure the length of the circumference to the nearest centimetre and label it.

Circumference

Use damp string to measure circumferences.

THINK About how many times the length of the diameter is the circumference of each circle?

○ **I am confident with labelling and measuring**
○ **parts of a circle.**
○

69

Draw and label a circle with:

GRAB! Damp string

1 a radius of 7·2 cm.

4 a radius of 4·8 cm.

2 a radius of 5·9 cm.

5 a radius of 6·7 cm.

3 a radius of 3·4 cm.

6 a radius of 8·1 cm.

Do the following for each of your circles.

7 Write the diameter.

Use damp string to measure circumferences.

8 Measure the length of the circumference as accurately as you can and label it.

Label the parts of this circle.

9

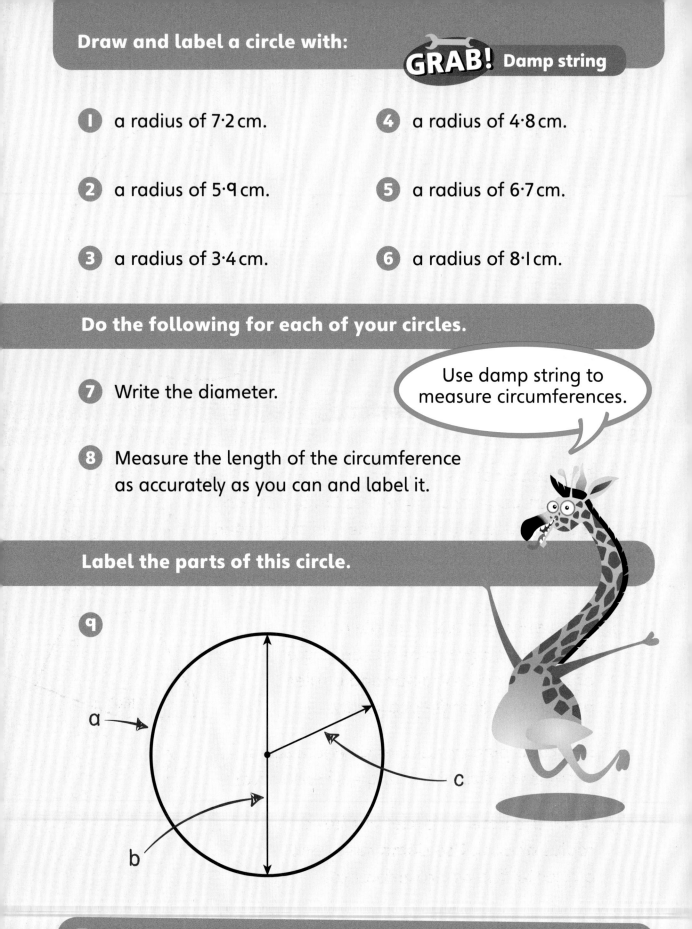

a

b

c

○ **I am confident with labelling and measuring parts of a circle.**

Use a ruler and a protractor to measure each of the following parts of this diagram:

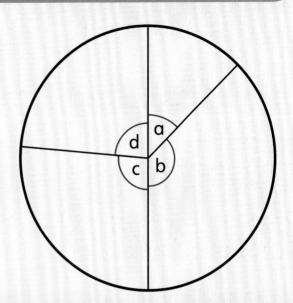

1. the diameter of this circle.

2. angle a

3. angle b

4. angle c

5. angle d

Answer the following questions about angles.

6. For each wash, the dial on a washing machine turns through a full turn. Mrs Smith puts on a wash. After 20 minutes the dial has turned through 120°. Through what angle will the dial turn now before the wash is finished?

7. This pentagon has an angle of 160°. Draw a pentagon that has an angle of 210°. Use a protractor and a ruler and draw the angle accurately.

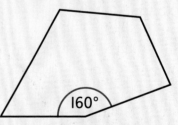

160°

8. A circular pizza is cut into six equal slices. What is the size of the angle of each slice?

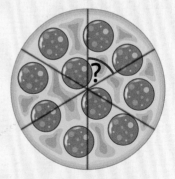

9. Draw accurately a circle that has a radius of 6 cm. Use damp string and a ruler to find its circumference.

○ **I am confident with measuring and drawing circles** ○ **and angles.**

1. the diameter of this circle.

2. angle a

3. angle b

4. angle c

5. angle d

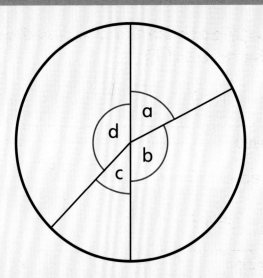

These pictures are not to scale. Answer the questions.

6. The diameter and radius are marked on this circle. Find the size of angle a. Do not use a protractor.

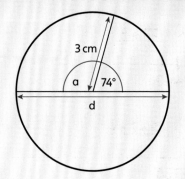

3 cm

a 74°

d

7. Find the length of the diameter d. Do not use a ruler.

8. Each circle has a radius of 5 cm and has its centre at the corner of a square. The square has sides of 10 cm. Draw an accurate drawing of the square and two circles. Use a ruler and a compass.

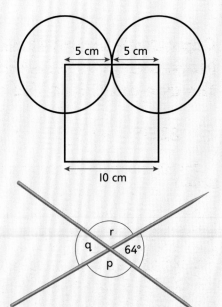

5 cm 5 cm

10 cm

9. Two kebab sticks lie crisscrossed on a table. This picture shows them. Without measuring, find the angles p, q and r.

r
q 64°
p

I am confident with measuring and drawing circles and angles.

Rounding 5-digit numbers

Copy each line and mark the given number. Then round it to the nearest 10.

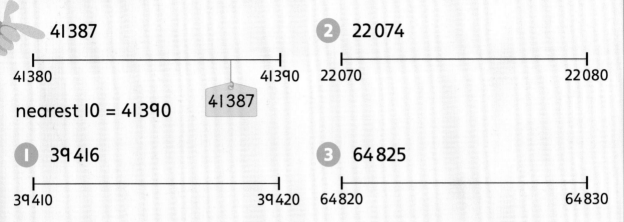

41387

41380   41390

41387

nearest 10 = 41390

2 22074

22070   22080

1 39416

39410   39420

3 64825

64820   64830

Copy each line and mark the given number. Then round it to the nearest 100.

4 27432

27400   27500

6 66159

66100   66200

5 45739

45700   45800

7 37061

37000   37100

Copy the line and table. Mark the given number on the line and fill in the table.

8 82715

82000   83000

82715	
Nearest 10	
Nearest 100	
Nearest 1000	

 Draw and complete a similar table for 68226.

- I am confident with placing 5-digit numbers on a number line and rounding them to the nearest 10, 100 and 1000.

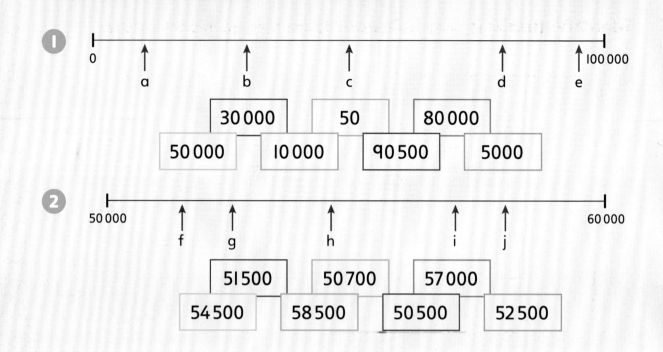

1

30 000		50		80 000	
50 000	10 000		90 500		5000

2

51 500		50 700		57 000
54 500	58 500		50 500	52 500

Copy the line and the table. Mark the given number on the line and fill in the table.

3 27 432

27 430 ———————————— 27 440

27 432	
Nearest 10	
Nearest 100	
Nearest 1000	

4 38 676

38 670 ———————————— 38 680

38 676	
Nearest 10	
Nearest 100	
Nearest 1000	

 **THINK** Draw and complete a similar table for 47 438.

I am confident with placing 5-digit numbers on a number line and rounding them to the nearest 10, 100 and 1000.

Rounding and ordering decimals

Identify numbers a to j. Choose from the numbers below.

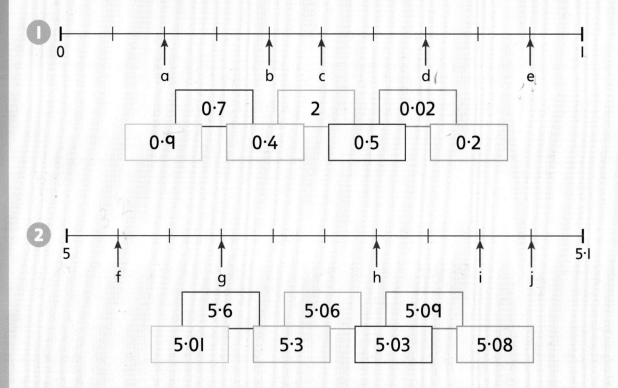

①

| 0.7 | 2 | 0.02 |

| 0.9 | 0.4 | 0.5 | 0.2 |

②

| 5.6 | 5.06 | 5.09 |

| 5.01 | 5.3 | 5.03 | 5.08 |

③ Draw a line from 5 to 6. Mark 5·6 and ring the nearest whole number.

④ Draw a line from 9 to 10. Mark 9·3 and ring the nearest whole number.

⑤ Draw a line from 3 to 4. Mark 3·45 and ring the nearest whole number.

⑥ Draw a line from 8 to 9. Mark 8·75 and ring the nearest whole number.

THINK Write some numbers that round to the whole number 6.

● I am confident with placing decimal numbers on
○ a number line and rounding them to the nearest
○ whole number.

Identify numbers a to t. Choose from the numbers below each line.

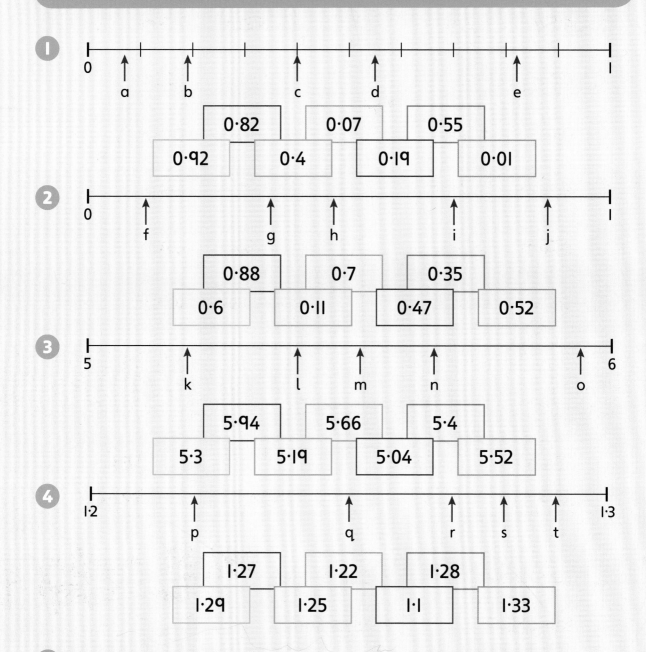

1

| | 0.82 | 0.07 | 0.55 | |
| 0.92 | 0.4 | | 0.19 | 0.01 |

2

| | 0.88 | 0.7 | 0.35 | |
| 0.6 | 0.11 | | 0.47 | 0.52 |

3

| | 5.94 | 5.66 | 5.4 | |
| 5.3 | 5.19 | | 5.04 | 5.52 |

4

| | 1.27 | 1.22 | 1.28 | |
| 1.29 | 1.25 | | 1.1 | 1.33 |

5 Draw a line from 7 to 8. Mark on 7·27 and ring the nearest whole number.

 **THINK** Draw a line from 3 to 4. Mark on two numbers, one which rounds to 3 and one which rounds to 4.

I am confident with placing decimal numbers on a number line and rounding them to the nearest whole number.

Write < or > between each pair of lengths.

1. 4·5 m   5·2 m

2. 0·7 m   1·1 m

3. 0·04 m   0·11 m

4. 6·34 m   6·42 m

5. 3·76 m   3·67 m

6. 6·6 m   6·06 m

7. 3·2 m   2·9 m

8. 12·4 m   1·25 m

9. 8·21 m   8·19 m

10. 0·75 m   0·8 m

11. 4·34 m   4·4 m

12. 10·75 m   10·8 m

**This table shows long jump distances.
Write who jumped further each time.**

Sam	Dan	Nia	Ed
2·63 m	2·9 m	3·05 m	3·2 m

13. Sam or Dan?

14. Nia or Ed?

15. Dan or Nia?

16. Ed or Sam?

Write a distance that lies between:

17. 3 m and 4 m.

18. 4·5 m and 4·6 m.

19. 3·02 m and 3·1 m.

●
○   **I am confident with comparing and ordering**
○   **decimal numbers.**

77

Name	Running time (s)	Swimming time (s)	Cycling time (s)
Sufia	12·34	39·48	27·4
Chang	12·4	40·25	27·03
Emma	12·37	39·9	28·2
Josh	12·45	40·1	28·05
Vijay	12·03	40·06	27·2
Scott	12·33	39·55	28·47
Kim	12·35	40·03	27·53

In each race who:

1. won?
2. came third?
3. came fifth?

4. came last?
5. came just after Emma?
6. came just before Josh?

7. What is the time difference between first and last in each race?

8. In the three races, who had the shortest overall time?

Write a number between:

9. 5·6 and 6·5.
10. 4·32 and 4·35.

11. 4·7 and 4·8.
12. 4·65 and 4·6.

13. 4·7 and 4·72.
14. 5 and 4·96.

THINK Using each of these digits only once in any number

4 7 0 6

make decimal numbers, either ☐·☐ or ☐·☐☐.

Investigate how many numbers you can make between 5 and 8. Put them in order.

● I am confident with comparing and ordering
○ decimal numbers.
○

comparing fractions and decimals

Write a fraction and a decimal for the part of each square that is coloured.

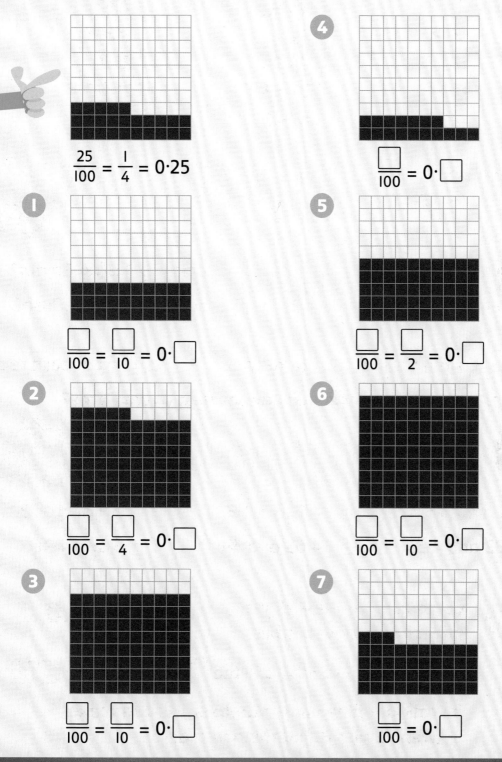

$$\frac{25}{100} = \frac{1}{4} = 0{\cdot}25$$

1

$$\frac{\square}{100} = \frac{\square}{10} = 0{\cdot}\square$$

2

$$\frac{\square}{100} = \frac{\square}{4} = 0{\cdot}\square$$

3

$$\frac{\square}{100} = \frac{\square}{10} = 0{\cdot}\square$$

4

$$\frac{\square}{100} = 0{\cdot}\square$$

5

$$\frac{\square}{100} = \frac{\square}{2} = 0{\cdot}\square$$

6

$$\frac{\square}{100} = \frac{\square}{10} = 0{\cdot}\square$$

7

$$\frac{\square}{100} = 0{\cdot}\square$$

○ **I am confident with recognising equivalent fractions**
○
○ **and decimals.**

Write a fraction and a decimal for the coloured part of each square. Write a simpler fraction if you can.

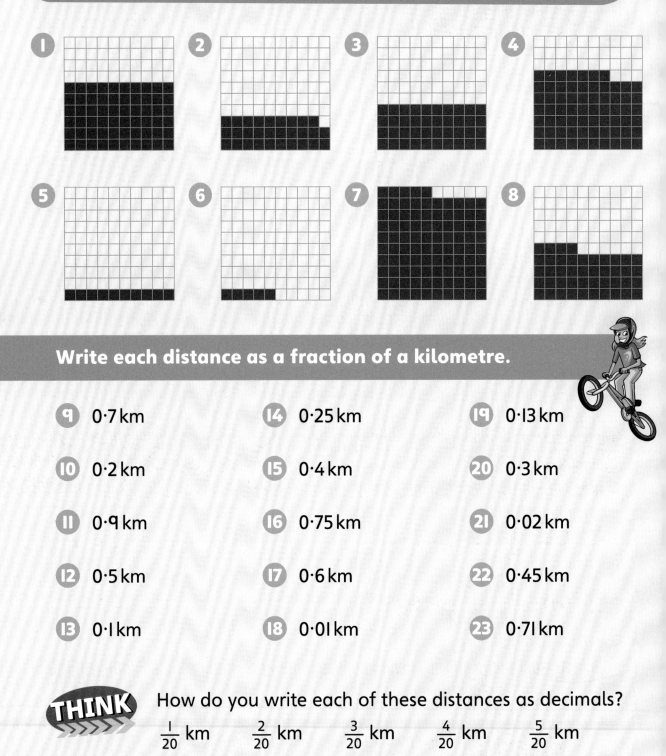

Write each distance as a fraction of a kilometre.

9 0·7 km

10 0·2 km

11 0·9 km

12 0·5 km

13 0·1 km

14 0·25 km

15 0·4 km

16 0·75 km

17 0·6 km

18 0·01 km

19 0·13 km

20 0·3 km

21 0·02 km

22 0·45 km

23 0·71 km

THINK How do you write each of these distances as decimals?

$\frac{1}{20}$ km $\frac{2}{20}$ km $\frac{3}{20}$ km $\frac{4}{20}$ km $\frac{5}{20}$ km

What patterns do you notice?

● **I am confident with recognising equivalent fractions**
○ **and decimals.**
○
○

Write each fraction as a decimal.

1. $\dfrac{31}{100}$
2. $\dfrac{9}{10}$
3. $\dfrac{3}{4}$
4. $\dfrac{1}{5}$
5. $\dfrac{1}{2}$

6. $\dfrac{3}{100}$
7. $\dfrac{11}{100}$
8. $\dfrac{3}{10}$
9. $\dfrac{4}{5}$
10. $\dfrac{3}{5}$

11. $\dfrac{1}{25}$
12. $\dfrac{1}{50}$
13. $\dfrac{1}{20}$
14. $\dfrac{3}{20}$
15. $\dfrac{7}{20}$

16. $\dfrac{2}{25}$
17. $\dfrac{99}{100}$
18. $\dfrac{3}{50}$
19. $\dfrac{8}{25}$
20. $\dfrac{24}{25}$

> Remember that $\dfrac{1}{10}$ is written as 0·1 and $\dfrac{1}{100}$ is written as 0·01. How many $\dfrac{1}{100}$s are the same as $\dfrac{1}{20}$? And as $\dfrac{1}{25}$?

Write each decimal as a fraction.
Write the fraction as simply as you can.

21. 0·31
22. 0·06
23. 0·79

24. 0·12
25. 0·45
26. 0·64

27. 0·95
28. 0·75
29. 0·4

30. 0·48
31. 0·2
32. 0·51

THINK Can you work out how the fractions $\dfrac{1}{3}$ and $\dfrac{2}{3}$ would be written as decimals?

I am confident with converting between fractions and decimals.

Addition and subtraction: mental strategies and written methods

Complete these 'no work' place-value additions.

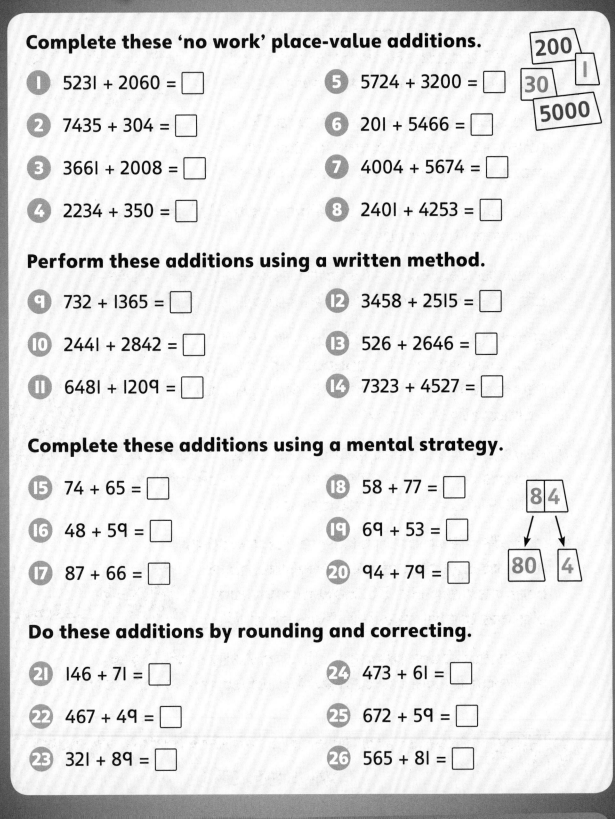

1. 5231 + 2060 = ☐
2. 7435 + 304 = ☐
3. 3661 + 2008 = ☐
4. 2234 + 350 = ☐

5. 5724 + 3200 = ☐
6. 201 + 5466 = ☐
7. 4004 + 5674 = ☐
8. 2401 + 4253 = ☐

200
30 1
5000

Perform these additions using a written method.

9. 732 + 1365 = ☐
10. 2441 + 2842 = ☐
11. 6481 + 1209 = ☐

12. 3458 + 2515 = ☐
13. 526 + 2646 = ☐
14. 7323 + 4527 = ☐

Complete these additions using a mental strategy.

15. 74 + 65 = ☐
16. 48 + 59 = ☐
17. 87 + 66 = ☐

18. 58 + 77 = ☐
19. 69 + 53 = ☐
20. 94 + 79 = ☐

84
80 4

Do these additions by rounding and correcting.

21. 146 + 71 = ☐
22. 467 + 49 = ☐
23. 321 + 89 = ☐

24. 473 + 61 = ☐
25. 672 + 59 = ☐
26. 565 + 81 = ☐

○
○
○
○
I am confident with adding using a variety of mental strategies and written methods.

1. At an ice rink there are 175 adults and 79 children. How many pairs of skates are needed for them in total?

2. In a computer game Ben scores 67 points in round one and 88 points in round two. How many points did he score altogether?

3. At a concert there are 3574 men and 6725 women. How many altogether?

4. A plane flies 3672 miles from one airport to another. It then flies 4783 miles to a third airport. How far did it fly?

5. On a train there are 267 passengers. It arrives at a station and 81 more passengers get on. No passengers get off the train. How many are on the train now?

6. Jamal has two lengths of wood. One is 68 cm long and the other is 74 cm. What is the length of them both if they are put end to end?

7. In 2008 AD an archaeologist discovered an Ancient Egyptian mask thought to have been made in 1321 BC. How many years old was the mask when it was found?

8. Jo has two bank accounts. In one there is £6411 and in the other there is £3020. How much has Jo in total?

 **THINK**   Make up your own word problem for this question:

$$4735 + 5623 = \boxed{}$$

I am confident with choosing an appropriate mental strategy or written method to perform an addition.

Do these 'no work' place-value subtractions.

1 7214 − 104 = ☐

2 4337 − 2004 = ☐

3 5986 − 640 = ☐

4 5789 − 4020 = ☐

5 A machine has made 7568 tennis balls. Of these balls 204 are faulty and are thrown away. How many are not thrown away?

Solve these subtractions using Frog.

6 664 − 589 = ☐

7 732 − 667 = ☐

8 3004 − 1979 = ☐

9 8012 − 6895 = ☐

10 Joe is cycling 224 km on a coast-to-coast route. He cycles 178 km on one day. How much further has he to go?

Solve these subtractions using a written method.

11 786 − 264 = ☐

12 2945 − 574 = ☐

13 6372 − 3458 = ☐

14 4786 − 2459 = ☐

15 Mr Patel has £8786 in a bank account. He spends £4527 of this money on a round-the-world trip. How much money does he have after the trip?

○ **I am confident with subtracting using various**
○
○ **mental and written methods.**

Complete these subtractions. Choose the most suitable mental or written method.

1. 5783 – 3040 = ☐

2. 4020 – 2985 = ☐

3. 453 – 82 = ☐

4. 9678 – 6879 = ☐

5. 4638 – 1007 = ☐

6. 7850 – 598 = ☐

7. 6893 – 2584 = ☐

8. 8075 – 5982 = ☐

9. 9011 – 3794 = ☐

10. 8305 – 7986 = ☐

11. 5675 – 2013 = ☐

12. 6784 – 3765 = ☐

Solve these word problems.

13. In the year 2033, how many years old will a person born in the year 1957 be?

14. On a train are 137 people. At the next station 78 people get off. How many people are on the train now?

15. A length of ribbon is 2500 mm. Jane cuts off a piece of ribbon with a length of 1235 mm. How much is left?

16. There are 2257 people at a rugby match. If 306 of them are children, how many are adults?

 Write four subtractions that are best solved using each of these methods:

| Frog | rounding | written method | 'no work' place value |

30 5
4000 100

I am confident with choosing an appropriate mental strategy or written method to perform a subtraction.

85

1. It is 3465 miles from London to New York. It is 5913 miles from London to Los Angeles, going via New York. How far is it from New York to Los Angeles?

2. On a plane there are 585 passengers, 198 of whom are children. How many are adults?

3. Jo has £3165 in a bank account. She withdraws £320 from the account. How much money is in the account now?

4. In the year 2029, how many years old will a person born in the year 1963 be?

5. A new ball of string is 1500 cm in length. Claire cuts off a piece that is 75 cm. She then cuts off another piece that is 320 cm long. How much string is left on the ball?

6. Hannah is climbing a mountain. Its summit is 2058 m above sea level. Hannah climbs to a height of 1894 m above sea level. How much higher above her is the summit?

7. Mount Everest is 8848 m tall. The height of Ben Nevis is 1344 m. How much taller is Mount Everest than Ben Nevis?

8. In the year 2019 there are 365 days. On 8 July, 189 days of the year have passed. How many days of the year remain?

I am confident with choosing an appropriate mental strategy or written method to perform a subtraction.

Multiplication and division: mental strategies and written methods

Use the grid method or another written method for these multiplications.

1 $56 \times 35 = \square$

2 $87 \times 42 = \square$

3 $758 \times 3 = \square$

4 $446 \times 8 = \square$

5 $389 \times 6 = \square$

6 $5327 \times 9 = \square$

Complete these multiplications mentally.

You can use jottings.

7 $78 \times 2 = \square$

8 $59 \times 4 = \square$

9 $342 \times 2 = \square$

10 $513 \times 4 = \square$

11 $51 \times 10 = \square$

12 $867 \times 10 = \square$

13 $46 \times 100 = \square$

14 $274 \times 100 = \square$

15 $34 \times 20 = \square$

16 $72 \times 20 = \square$

17 $365 \times 20 = \square$

18 $528 \times 20 = \square$

Solve these problems mentally or with a written method.

19 A shop sold 20 computers, each costing £485. How much money did they get?

20 Each crate in a drinks factory holds 27 bottles. How many bottles in 32 crates?

● I am confident with using various mental or written
○ methods to perform a multiplication.
○

1 87 × 2 = ☐

2 69 × 4 = ☐

3 463 × 2 = ☐

4 785 × 10 = ☐

5 67 × 20 = ☐

6 84 × 5 = ☐

7 46 × 100 = ☐

8 274 × 6 = ☐

9 3435 × 7 = ☐

10 742 × 16 = ☐

11 32 × 15 = ☐

12 73 × 25 = ☐

Solve these problems mentally or with a written method.

13 Each day a factory makes 1752 cars. How many does it make in one week, working for 7 days a week?

14 How many horseshoes are needed for 74 horses?

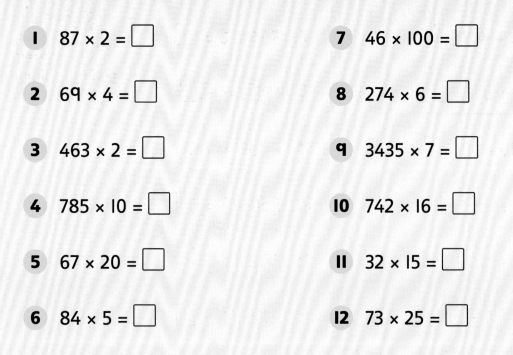

15 In a tournament each football team has 24 players. There are 16 teams in the tournament. How many players are there altogether?

16 A tin of beans costs 59p. How much would it cost to buy 20 of them?

 Which is shorter?
7 × 662 cm or 6 × 772 cm

 I am confident with choosing a mental or written method to perform a multiplication.

Use a mental or written method for these divisions.

1 $484 \div 4 = \square$

2 $195 \div 5 = \square$

3 $4030 \div 10 = \square$

4 $128 \div 2 = \square$

5 $276 \div 6 = \square$

6 $126 \div 3 = \square$

7 $344 \div 8 = \square$

8 $156 \div 4 = \square$

9 $4000 \div 100 = \square$

10 $266 \div 7 = \square$

11 $396 \div 9 = \square$

12 $672 \div 6 = \square$

Solve these problems mentally or with a written method.

13 There are 7 days in a week. How many weeks are the same as 252 days?

14 There are 10 mm in 1 cm. How many centimetres are the same as 740 mm?

15 At a school sports day some oranges are cut into quarters for the pupils. How many oranges were there if there are 264 quarters?

16 Eggs come in boxes of 6. How many boxes are needed for 522 eggs?

I am confident with choosing a mental or written method to perform a division.

89

Use a mental or written method for these divisions.
Give any remainders as fractions.

1 485 ÷ 6 = ☐

2 437 ÷ 5 = ☐

3 6700 ÷ 10 = ☐

4 143 ÷ 2 = ☐

5 673 ÷ 6 = ☐

6 369 ÷ 3 = ☐

7 679 ÷ 8 = ☐

8 864 ÷ 4 = ☐

9 52 000 ÷ 100 = ☐

10 406 ÷ 7 = ☐

11 777 ÷ 2 = ☐

12 927 ÷ 9 = ☐

Solve these problems mentally or with a written method.

13 Eggs come in boxes of six. How many boxes are needed for 477 eggs?

14 How many pairs can be made from 473 identical socks?

15 At a restaurant each pizza is cut into six slices. If 282 slices were served one evening, how many whole pizzas was this?

 Write a mental and a written division. How did you decide what numbers to use? What rules did you use to write them?

●
● **I am confident with choosing a mental or written**
● **method to perform a division.**

Identifying operations

Work out the function for each machine.

1.
137 → → 1370
45·5 → → 455
0·6 → → 6

2.
24 → → 74
243 → → 293
3839 → → 3889

3.
573 → → 553
4824 → → 4804
23·5 → → 3·5

Write the input numbers for each output.

4. ☐ → → 74
5. ☐ → → 272
6. ☐ → → 698
7. ☐ → → 143
8. ☐ → → 477

(machine shows ÷ 2)

I am confident with identifying the correct operation performed by a function machine.

Work out the function for each machine.

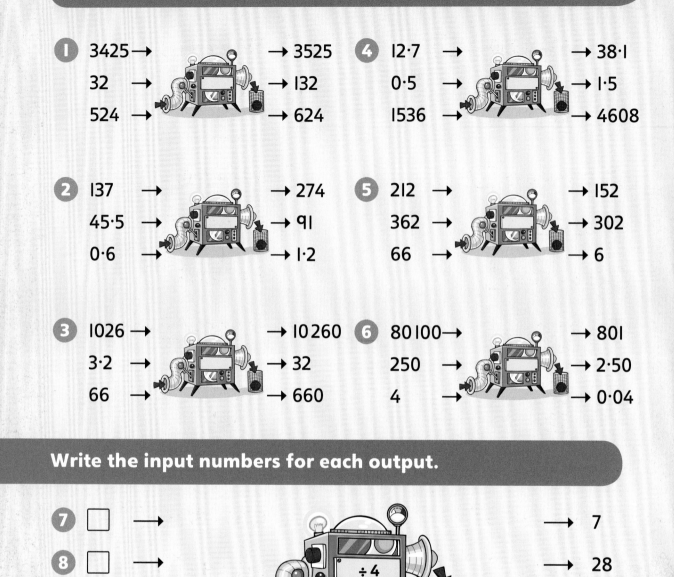

1
3425 → → 3525
32 → → 132
524 → → 624

4
12·7 → → 38·1
0·5 → → 1·5
1536 → → 4608

2
137 → → 274
45·5 → → 91
0·6 → → 1·2

5
212 → → 152
362 → → 302
66 → → 6

3
1026 → → 10 260
3·2 → → 32
66 → → 660

6
80 100 → → 801
250 → → 2·50
4 → → 0·04

Write the input numbers for each output.

7 ☐ → ÷ 4 → 7

8 ☐ → → 28

9 ☐ → → 698

10 ☐ → × 5 → 105

11 ☐ → → 360

12 ☐ → → 1245

○ **I am confident with identifying the correct operation**
○ **performed by a function machine.**
○

92

Practising calculations

1 45 834 + 3004 = ☐

2
```
   7667
+   514
_____
```

3 0·63 − 0·1 = ☐

4 52 × 25 = ☐

5 116 − 88 = ☐

6
```
   2000
− 1978
```

7
```
   816
− 339
```

8 352 ÷ 8 = ☐

9 7850 − 598 = ☐

10 276 ÷ 6 = ☐

11 260 ÷ 7 = ☐

12
```
   4543
+ 7258
_____
```

13 0·29 + 0·01 = ☐

14 7 × 7859 = ☐

15 321 − 284 = ☐

16 292 275 − ☐ = 82 175

17
```
   932
− 533
```

18 3735 × 3 = ☐

19 6784 − 3765 = ☐

20 396 ÷ 9 = ☐

21 There are 7 days in a week. How many weeks are the same as 252 days?

22 In the year 2033, how many years old will a person born in the year 1959 be?

23 The tallest man ever to live, Robert Wadlow, was 272 cm. Ryan is 96 cm shorter than this. How tall is Ryan?

24 A coat was reduced in a sale by £47. If it cost £81 before the sale, what was its sale price?

Number puzzles

The numbers in each row of shapes follow the same pattern. Each shape should have a number in it.

Row 1: △ 78, □, ○, ⬡ 292

Row 2: △ 93, □, ○, ⬡ 307

Row 3: △ 56, □, ○, ⬡

Row 4: △ 67, □, ○, ⬡

1 Copy this diagram.

2 Work out and fill in the missing numbers so that, in each row these are the patterns:

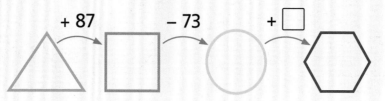

△ +87→ □ −73→ ○ +□→ ⬡

3 What is the difference between △ and ○ in each row?

4 What is the difference between ○ and ⬡ in each row?

5 Draw one more row in your diagram. Choose any starting number you like and fill in the numbers.

6 This row follows the same patterns. Can you work out the missing numbers?

△, □, ○ 25, ⬡

This puzzle has a different set of rules to the previous page.

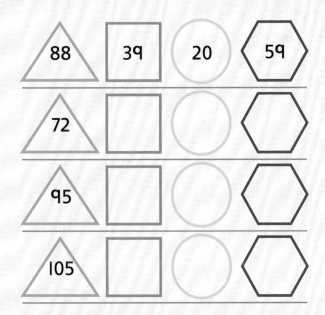

88	39	20	59
72			
95			
105			

7 Use the first row to work out the rules.

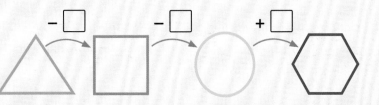

$-\square$ $-\square$ $+\square$

8 Now use your rules to copy and complete the diagram above.

9 Can you arrange the digits 1 to 9 to make a correct addition question and answer? Only use each digit once.

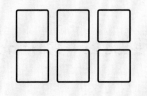

+

Clue: Start with the 1s digits 7 and 4.

How many different answers can you find?

Series Editor
Ruth Merttens

Author Team
Jennie Kerwin and Hilda Merttens

Published by Pearson Education Limited, Edinburgh Gate, Harlow, Essex, CM20 2JE.

www.pearsonschools.co.uk

Text © Pearson Education Limited 2013
Typeset by Debbie Oatley @ room9design
Original illustrations © Pearson Education Limited 2013
Illustrated by Matthew Buckley, Marek Jagucki, Anthony Rule, Debbie Oatley
Cover design by Pearson Education Limited
Cover photo/illustration by Volker Beisler © Pearson Education Limited

First published 2013

16 15 14
10 9 8 7 6 5 4 3

British Library Cataloguing in Publication Data
A catalogue record for this book is available from the British Library

ISBN 978 1 408 27853 6

Copyright notice
All rights reserved. No part of this publication may be reproduced in any form or by any means (including photocopying or storing it in any medium by electronic means and whether or not transiently or incidentally to some other use of this publication) without the written permission of the copyright owner, except in accordance with the provisions of the Copyright, Designs and Patents Act 1988 or under the terms of a licence issued by the Copyright Licensing Agency, Saffron House, 6–10 Kirby Street, London EC1N 8TS (www.cla.co.uk). Applications for the copyright owner's written permission should be addressed to the publisher.

Printed in Slovakia by Neografia

Acknowledgements
We would like to thank the staff and pupils at North Kidlington Primary School, Haydon Wick Primary School, Swindon, St Mary's Catholic Primary School, Bodmin, St Andrew's C of E Primary & Nursery School, Sutton-in-Ashfield, Saint James' C of E Primary School, Southampton and Harborne Primary School, Birmingham, for their invaluable help in the development and trialling of this book.

Every effort has been made to contact copyright holders of material reproduced in this book. Any omissions will be rectified in subsequent printings if notice is given to the publishers.